Quilt National 2003

the best of contemporary quilts

Quilt National 2003

the best of contemporary quilts

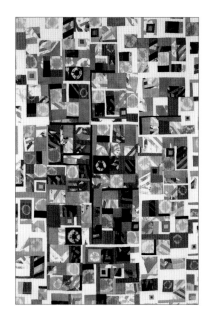

Coproduced by

Lark Books & the Dairy Barn Cultural Arts Center

LARK BOOKS

A Division of Sterling Publishing Co., Inc.
New York

Quilt National Project Director: Hilary Morrow Fletcher
Editor: Dawn Cusick
Art Director: Megan Kirby
Photographer: Brian Blauser
Cover Designer: Barbara Zaretsky
Production Assistance: Lorelei Buckley

Additional photography provided by Hester & Hardaway (page 9), David Loveall Photography, Inc. (page 10), D. James Dee (page 23), Kyoung Ae Cho (page 30), Jay Yocis (page 32), Bruno Jarret (page 33), Gene Balzer (page 38), Sam Newbury (page 46), Geoffrey Nilsen (page 47), Ken Sanville (page 49), Karen Bell (page 50), Sharon Risedorph (page 51), Larry Gawel (page 53), Sharon Risedorph (page 54), Eric Kievit (page 64), Gulezian/QuickSilver (page 65), James Dewrance (page 67), David Belda (page 78), Mark Gulezian (page 82), Gregory Gantner (page 92), PRS Associates, Inc. (page 93), Karen Bell (page 97), Nancy N. Erickson (page 107).

Library of Congress Cataloging-in-Publication Data

Quilt National (2003 : Athens, Ohio)
  Quilt National 2003 : the best of contemporary quilts / editor: Dawn Cusick.
      p. cm.
"Coproduced by Lark Books and the Dairy Barn Cultural Arts Center."
Includes index.
  ISBN 1-57990-503-X
  1. Art quilts—United States—History—20th century—Exhibitions. 2.
Art quilts—History—20th century—Exhibitions. I. Cusick, Dawn. II.
Lark Books. III. Dairy Barn Southeastern Ohio Cultural Arts Center. IV. Title.
  NK9112.Q5 2003
  746.46'0973'07477197—dc21
                          2003000518

10 9 8 7 6 5 4 3 2 1

First Edition

Published by Lark Books, a division of
Sterling Publishing Co., Inc.
387 Park Avenue South, New York, N.Y. 10016

© 2003, Lark Books

Distributed in Canada by Sterling Publishing,
c/o Canadian Manda Group, One Atlantic Ave., Suite 105
Toronto, Ontario, Canada M6K 3E7

Distributed in the U.K. by Guild of Master Craftsman Publications Ltd.,
Castle Place, 166 High Street, Lewes, East Sussex, England BN7 1XU
Tel: (+ 44) 1273 477374, Fax: (+ 44) 1273 478606,
Email: pubs@thegmcgroup.com, Web: www.gmcpublications.com

Distributed in Australia by Capricorn Link (Australia) Pty Ltd.,
P.O. Box 704, Windsor, NSW 2756 Australia

The works of art in this book are the original creations of the contributing artists who created them; the artists retain full copyrights to them.

Every effort has been made to ensure that all the information in this book is accurate. However, due to differing conditions, tools, and individual skills, the publisher cannot be responsible for any injuries, losses, and other damages that may result from the use of the information in this book.

If you have questions or comments about this book, please contact:
Lark Books, 67 Broadway, Asheville, NC 28801, (828) 236-9730

Printed in Hong Kong

ISBN 1-57990-503-X

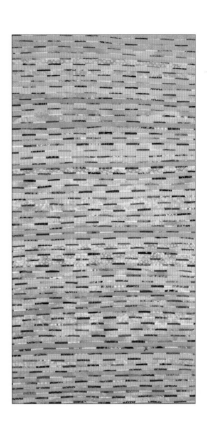

Contents

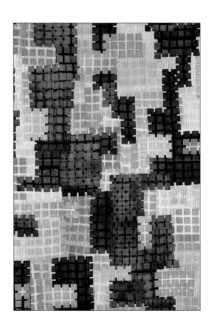

Foreword

It might sound clichéd to say Quilt National is a labor of love, but in this case, it's true.

This is the 13th biennial Quilt National, a unique exhibition designed to stimulate the growing art quilt and fiber arts audiences. Project Director Hilary Morrow Fletcher has, over the past 22 years, sustained and enhanced this exhibition through her steadfast devotion to Quilt National, *the* showcase of contemporary quilts.

Who would have dreamed that an exhibition in Athens, Ohio, would develop into the world-class exhibition we have today? They say imitation is the best form of flattery, and we are gratified that so many art quilt exhibits have been spawned by Quilt National.

We wish to thank those who helped make this beautiful exhibition and book possible.

First, we must thank the many artists who submitted work, making the job of this year's jury a tough one. You'll want to read the thoughtful statement prepared by Liz Axford, Wendy Huhn, and Robert Shaw about the jurying process. We offer many thanks to them for the hours they devoted to selecting this year's show, and hope they enjoyed the experience as much as we did.

Many thanks to Hilary Fletcher, Maria Medina López, other Dairy Barn staff and volunteers, exhibition designer Ann Moneypenny, and photographer Brian Blauser, all of whom make this remarkable exhibition shine.

We are also grateful for the vision and guidance provided by Carol Taylor, Director of Publishing, Editor Dawn Cusick and Art Director Megan Kirby, of Lark Books, in producing this book.

Although Athens is your only opportunity to see Quilt National in its entirety, parts of the show are available to travel to venues throughout the country. For more information, call 740-592-4981, visit our website at www.dairybarn.org, or e-mail: artsinfo@dairybarn.org.

I invite you to visit the Dairy Barn during this and other exhibitions or programs. You won't be disappointed!

Krista Campbell
Executive Director
Dairy Barn Cultural Arts Center

An exhibition of this quality would not be possible without the financial support of our sponsors. Major support is provided by Fairfield Processing Corporation, maker of Poly-fil brand fiber products. Additional support comes from Quilts Japan Magazine, Bernina of America, the James Foundation, Friends of Fiber Art International, FreeSpirit Fabrics, Studio Art Quilt Associates, the Ohio Arts Council, the City of Athens, and other generous individuals and businesses.

Introduction

What is Quilt National? You may think you know the answer to this question: Quilt National is a biennial international juried exhibition of innovative quilts that are shown in Athens, Ohio, at the Dairy Barn Cultural Arts Center during the summer of odd-numbered years. That answer, although accurate, is far from being complete. The quilts are only the tip of the iceberg. The reality is that Quilt National is time and people.

Quilt National is history. Although the originality of the QN works was shockingly unacceptable for some, the truth is that QN exhibitors were and are doing exactly what generations of their predecessors have done. They are using their creativity and a variety of old and new techniques to shape available materials into objects using images that may or may not be immediately understandable. Every familiar classic quilt design from Abe Lincoln's Platform to Zinnia Applique was once the original creation of a single anonymous quiltmaker who most likely would not have identified herself as an artist.

If one were to compare the images in this book with the documentation of earlier Quilt Nationals, the increasing distance between the center of the quilt world and the boundaries of the art form would be obvious; and yet, there is still a connection between them. There has always been a symbiotic relationship between the classic quilted bedcover and the nonfunctional art quilt. The work by John Lefelhocz (see page 87), for instance, is a clear reflection of a classic quilt design, albeit one that is executed in materials that are anything but classic. At the same time, many once cutting-edge techniques are showing up with increasing frequency in local guild shows: intricately patterned machine quilting; surface embellishment with embroidery, found objects, and even paint; fabrics that are actual or simulated hand-dyes; and even photographic and computer-generated images. It gives me great pleasure to know that the Quilt National "pebble" has had such a broad ripple effect on the larger quilting community.

The other temporal aspect of Quilt National is that it's a never-ending process. The debut of the QN '03 collection will likely coincide with a host venue's exhibition of works from QN' 01; and almost as soon as crates of QN'03 quilts leave the Dairy Barn, the jurors for QN '05 will be contacted.

Each QN is planned with a ten-page, single-spaced time line that includes items like "contact post office for new regulations that may impact the design decisions for the entry forms," or "research shops, guilds, and events for distribution of call-for-entry flyers." Hopefully, the exhibition has been facilitated and enhanced by my administrative continuity.

Someone once called me a "Master of Minutiae." The fact is, however, that any project like Quilt National requires attention to an enormous number of details because the interests of so many different groups of people must always be considered. There is no question in my mind that people are absolutely the most important element of Quilt National.

The entrants are, of course, Quilt National's *raison d'etre*. What began in 1979 as an exhibit opportunity for quilt-makers whose works didn't fit the standards of the day, is now a prize sought by fiber artists from all over the world.

It would be impossible to mount an exhibition without funding. The generosity of the sponsors mentioned in this book's foreword provides invaluable support for the activities of the Dairy Barn's staff and corps of volunteers. One of my top priorities is to ensure that Quilt National continues to be a source of pride for those whose corporate and individual names are associated with it.

Creating Quilt National has always been a team effort. Some, like photographer Brian Blauser and exhibition designer Ann Moneypenny, have been on board almost from the beginning. Throughout the years they have been joined by nearly 40 jurors and a loyal and dedicated group of volunteers whose endless gifts of time and talent continue to amaze me. I simply cannot imagine there being a Quilt National without them.

We haven't yet reached the point where everyone knows about Quilt National. That's why the editors, managers, and writers for general interest and specialty publications, as well as internet sites, are such an important component in the recipe for QN's success. They aid in increasing the visibility of the program for potential entrants as well as visitors. The efforts of those who actually produce QN would be futile if others didn't learn about it.

Jurors' Statement

The last, largest, and probably most significant group of QN people are those who visit the show at one of the display venues (or through the pages of this book.) While the vast majority are thrilled with the exhibitions, there are always a few who are reluctant attendees. These few are like I was in 1978, when I thought that all quilts were boring repetitions of someone else's ideas.

My first visit to QN '79 provided conclusive evidence that all my ideas about quilts were wrong. I became a convert to quilts — and with the development of computer-assisted design software — to quilting. Since then, my passion for quilts has grown and I admit to sometimes being over-zealous in my efforts to encourage others to join my two-decade-long crusade to foster an appreciation, if not love, of ALL kinds of quilts. By sharing information about the who/why/and how of the Quilt National works, I hope visitors will gain an understanding of the quilts. Even if they are not drawn to the imagery of some of the pieces, I would like our visitors to appreciate the creativity and skills necessary to create them.

Being the project director of Quilt National provides me many satisfactions. By far, the most meaningful of these is watching the growth of the legions of quilt lovers who, over time, will appreciate the depth and breadth of all that the words Quilt National encompass. The music I enjoy most are the words, "That was wonderful. We'll see you again in two years!"

As you study the images in this book, I hope you'll decide to join my crusade. And while you're at it, why not bring someone else along with you?

Hilary Morrow Fletcher
Quilt National Project Director

Jurying Quilt National, the gold standard of contemporary quilt exhibitions, is both an honor and a serious responsibility. When Quilt National Director Hilary Fletcher called Liz to ask if she would be a juror, she posed the question as, "How would you like to lose all of your friends?" Hilary was joking, of course, but her point is well taken. Our job as jurors would be to leave our friends and preconceived notions behind, and bring all our critical skills to the work that had been submitted.

Quilt National continues to break its own record of number of entries, with 1452 works (by 676 artists from 47 states and 20 countries!) submitted this year. Including overalls and details, that translated to 38 carousels filled with nearly 80 slides each. Our hats are off to Hilary and her highly organized staff. We could not have done our job without them. A dedicated team of volunteers was there all weekend to project slides, read titles and sizes, answer questions about materials and techniques, tabulate scores, and rearrange slides in carousels. It was a huge undertaking. We also enjoyed some terrific meals (and many cups of coffee) in the adjoining conference room, again courtesy of the volunteers. Thank you all for making a difficult task enjoyable and efficient.

We arrived in Athens on a Friday night and viewed all of the quilts that evening. We made no decisions that night; instead, we simply looked at the overall view of each quilt for approximately five seconds each to get a sense of the territory without knowing anything about the makers, the materials, or the techniques. The entire viewing took just under two hours. Our minds were reeling by the end of this onslaught of images, which one former juror described as the visual equivalent of being run over by an 18 wheeler. The following morning, we looked at the slides again. A volunteer called out the entrant's number and A, B, or C for the first, second or third quilt by that artist, the title of each piece, and its dimensions, allowing us to identify a small body of work for each entrant.

Next we began the elimination process. This time we looked at each pair of slides (a quilt and its detail) for approximately 20 seconds. No discussion was permitted, though some of the pieces prompted us to ask questions about the technique and/or materials. Each juror had an independent set of score sheets on which he or she assigned a score ranging from 1 through 4 for each quilt. As each sheet was completed, it was quickly whisked away by a volunteer. In another room, the scores were tabulated to determine which quilts would advance to the next round. This stage of the jurying process took almost six hours and eliminated approximately 50 percent of the quilts. What did we look for in this first round? Good composition, good color, some sense of content or theme, and a coherent body of work from each entrant. For a juried show with work selected by slides, the role of photography cannot be overstated. Slides that were poorly exposed (too light/too dark), out of focus, or shot against distracting backgrounds (including beds, barns, clotheslines, hands and feet, pastoral scenery, and impressively green grass) were problematic and had to be eliminated. Our advice: Shoot your quilt against a plain white or black background.

A number of themes seemed to be in the air: Skeletons (we're afraid this show will be known as "The Skeleton Show"), animals (especially cats), circles (often hollow ones, clearly made using surplus CDs), nudes, mummies, and goddesses. As we'd expected, surface design played a large part in many of the works. We were surprised there weren't more improvisational quilts based on traditional patterns. We looked at the remaining slides twice more that Saturday, eliminating approximately half each time. The last round that day sought to eliminate more quilts, and specifically, duplicate quilts by the same artist. At this point we were allowed, for the first time, discussion on quilts by the same artist to reach a consensus on which quilt, if any, of the remaining multiple entries would continue to the next round. By the end of the day, we were left with 163 quilts by 163 artists. Although we had never worked together before, we all know and respect each other's work, and we found that respect translated easily into a true team approach. No one juror dominated the proceedings, and we listened hard to each other's opinions and questions. We were pleasantly surprised that we were all equally committed to a majority

Liz Axford

Life Lines 1
Invitational Work: Quilt National 2003 Juror
Whole-cloth quilt of silk/wool gauze; pattern created with orinui (stitched) shibori, dyed in Procian MX; layered with cotton batting and hand-dyed silk broadcloth, quilted with silk buttonhole twist; 40 x 72 inches (102 x 183 cm).

While studying and practicing architecture, I learned to use linear and planar shapes to create space. I try to do the same in my quiltmaking. My current work relies on shibori, a Japanese resist dyeing technique, to create the composition.

of the quilts that were ultimately accepted into the show. In all cases where we did not agree, two of us were passionate about the work and did their best to persuade the reluctant one.

We began the second day with a review of the remaining 163 quilts. We were generally pleased with what we saw, and we felt the show could take shape in many different ways. Also at this point we wanted to make sure that any assumptions we had about specific quilts were true. We were now able to ask for confirmation of the maker, for example: "Is this piece by Shie and Acord?" If not, we assumed it was the product of a student or an admirer, and should most likely be eliminated from the viewing. By the way, having a recognizable style is a double-edged sword: It was impossible for us not to consider how a piece fits into the artist's known *oeuvre* and ask whether it covers new territory or is a rehash of old ideas. Does it disappoint, somehow, in contrast to past accomplishments? Not all work by known artists could be recognized, however we were pleased to find such well-known artists as Michael James, Miriam Nathan-Roberts, Patty Hawkins, Connie Scheele, Erika Carter, Allison Whitmore, and Dominie Nash each working in new and sometimes surprising ways.

In these last rounds, considerations of appropriate size, scale, and workmanship also became more important. In general, we preferred big quilts because they display a real commitment on the part of the maker, and because they connect more easily to the traditions of quiltmaking. Small works demand a sense of intimacy in all ways. We felt many of them would work better if they were larger. After considering design and content, we chose work that we felt showed better workmanship. And for that we relied on good slide details, details that gave a sense of the techniques and the quality of construction. Some details showed almost as much area as the overall. Ideally, a detail should zero in on a small area — no more than 12 inches (30 cm) in the long direction. Really good details are engaging by themselves and draw you back into the overall shot for another look. Details must also be consistent with the overall shot. One piece was elim-

Wendy Huhn

Silent Killer
Invitational Work: Quilt National 2003 Juror
Printed canvas, photocopied fabric, acrylic paints, couching/ribbons, horsehair netting, doll hair, vintage apron, sequins, and beads; machine quilted with monofilament; 64 x 72 inches (163 x 183 cm).

Hemochromatosis, also known as Iron Overload Disorder. The first time I heard this term was in 1998 when I was diagnosed. In a nutshell: IOD is the hereditary iron overloading of vital organs and joints. Left untreated, it can literally rust the body to death. How do you know if you have it? Typically someone in your family dies and IOD is discovered upon autopsy. This person is known as the "sacrificial sibling." A simple blood test can determine if you are at risk. Symptoms may vary from anemia to chronic fatigue. This is most commonly an undiagnosed treatable disorder, meaning you don't have to die. Treatment? In past centuries it was simple: leeches. Now phlebotomies are used to rapidly reduce iron. In making this quilt I hope to educate the viewer through humor to be tested so hemochromatosis will no longer bear the name of Silent Killer.

inated in the later rounds because the overall and detail shots were completely different colors: one had rich color, while the other appeared faded. Because we were not confident that we truly understood what the quilt looked like, we had to eliminate it.

Some entries had painted surfaces, and we struggled over these as we examined the techniques and details closely. We ended up eliminating several pieces that struck us as quilted paintings, works where we questioned why the artist had chosen the quilt medium instead of canvas or felt because the minimal quilting did not add anything to the composition. Before we were allowed a final viewing of the slides, with names revealed, we were asked to view all of the entry slides again — this time on the light table. Could a quilt worthy of inclusion have somehow slipped by? Was there anything we wanted to see projected one more time? To our surprise, we selected a half dozen quilts to be projected again. In all but one case our judgments were remembered and confirmed; in that last case, we added a quilt, a multiple entry by a maker whose alternate entry had been eliminated in the last round. This new choice satisfied us in a way that the other quilt had, in the end, failed to. A volunteer inserted the slide in the remaining carousels. We had selected the show.

Having winnowed a show of 84 quilts from the original 1452 entries, we could now begin choosing award winners. We were surprisingly united on those choices. Nancy Erickson's *Felis Forever (1)* spoke to us on a gut level — the cat just took command of the screen on day one and stayed with us throughout the weekend. We hope he will also take command of the Dairy Barn and wonder if his eyes will follow us as we move around the quilt. We can't wait to see Nancy's quilt in person. Ludmila Uspenskaya's *Recharge,* recipient of the Award of Excellence, also has a powerful presence, with a strong overall composition and sense of scale more typical of paintings. Her rich colors and varied textures envelop the viewer in a way that only a quilt can. The *Quilts Japan* Prize was also an easy choice. Because the winner will be flown to Japan by Quilts Japan magazine to teach and lecture, the recipient needs to be accomplished in both areas.

Elizabeth Busch's *Abundance* represents a fresh approach to her particular brand of surface design and quilting; she is also a superb teacher and an articulate speaker.

There were relatively few entries that pushed the boundaries of what we think of as quilts or focused on using materials in an innovative way. We chose Michael James' *A Strange Riddle* for the Most Innovative Use of the Medium Award because it predicts a world of things yet to come — the increasing use of computer generated/manipulated imagery in surface design. We also felt Michael was very successful in integrating his digitally printed fabric with more conventional textiles. We gave the Lynn Goodwin Borgman Award for Surface Design to Clare Plug from Australia. In *Nocturne in G,* she has created a intriguingly ambiguous surface, full of color nuances and illusions of depth. This is a perfect example of the use of surface design techniques in service of a well-integrated overall composition. Bean Gilsdorf's *Ouija 1,* recipient of the Cathy Rasmussen Emerging Artist Memorial Prize, grabbed us the first time we saw it. It is part of a strong and edgy body of work that deserves more attention; Bean is an artist whose work we expect to see much more of. Nelda Warkentin's *Tropical Dream,* which receives the Dominie McCarthy Memorial Award, is also part of a deep body of work. It relies on the repetition of two simple, large-scale blocks, rendered with many layers of painted sheer fabric and stitched on an industrial machine, resulting in a lush, complex, and evocative surface.

After choosing the award winners, we sat down to view the slides one more time. Now, for the first time, all the makers' names were revealed to us. We were surprised by how many newcomers had been accepted to the show. Almost 46 percent of the makers had never been included in a previous Quilt National. Some were known to us, many more were not. We were delighted by the number of foreign entries that were accepted; this is truly an international exhibit.

We were also surprised by how many quiltmakers of reputation and stature did not seem to be included. Had they not entered or had their entries failed to catch or keep our attention? Since the makers of the unchosen works remain anonymous to us, we will never know. What we do know is that this show represents a snapshot of the best of contemporary quiltmaking, as chosen by a panel of mere mortals on the third weekend of September of 2002. Jurying is by definition subjective. We recognize that a different panel of jurors, or even the three of us at a different time, would likely have chosen a somewhat different show. We are confident that most of the pieces would be the same; but a few others would probably be replaced by quilts equally worthy of consideration.

To all those who entered, thank you. The high quality of your work made our job difficult. It is gratifying to see how many artists have made the commitment to quiltmaking as their medium. We encourage all of you to keep working. Try new ideas, learn from others, but keep seeking your own voice. And when you've found that voice, and your work reflects it, take excellent slides, or, better yet, hire a professional to do it. If you feel like you are already "there," take heart and just keep going. If you feel you have been overlooked, reconsider your position, then press on. If your work is strong, it surely will be recognized in the future.

We hope that the exhibition we have chosen not only documents the current state of the art, but also contributes to its evolution. It is our hope that you will look hard at the quilts, as we did, debate our choices, and reach your own conclusions. Most of all, we hope you will enjoy the show.

Liz Axford, Wendy Huhn, and Robert Shaw,
Quilt National 2003 Jurors

Liz Axford lives and works in Houston, Texas. Having practiced architecture for almost ten years, she became a full-time quiltmaker in 1985. Her work has been included in many juried shows including Quilt National, Crafts National, Fiberarts International, and Materials: Hard and Soft. She was the 1998 recipient of the Visions Quilt Japan Prize, and in 2001 was chosen to be one of five inaugural Visiting Artists at the Houston Center for Contemporary Craft.

Wendy Huhn maintains a studio in Dexter, Oregon. She is best known for her mixed media textiles that blend together a history of imagery and surface design techniques to create a visual language. Teaching venues include: the University of Oregon, Arrowmont, Penland, Truman Sate University, Kansas City Art Institute, and the Textile Museum in the Netherlands. Her work is included in many public and private collections including the American Craft Museum, the George Stroemple Collection, and the Children's Receiving Center.

Robert Shaw is one of the country's leading authorities on traditional American crafts and folk arts. His 1997 book *The Art Quilt* was the first comprehensive overview of the history and achievements of the new medium. He also authored *Quilts: A Living Tradition, Hawaiian Quilt Masterpieces, America's Traditional Crafts, Great Guitars,* and *American Baskets.* He lectures frequently on quilts and other traditional arts, curates exhibitions, and serves as a consultant to collectors, museums, and auction houses worldwide.

The Quilts

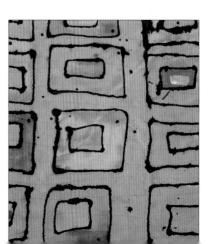

Bethan Ash
Cardiff, Wales,
United Kingdom

Cell-U-Lite
Hand-dyed and painted silk, satin
and cotton fabrics; machine
stitched (after fusing) and
machine quilted; 36 x 68 inches
(91 x 173 cm).

Inspiration for the patterns
used in *Cell-U-Lite* came from
photographs of cell structures
and fabric wastage from other
quilt projects. The title came
from my constant battle against
cellulite. I have never
approached quiltmaking as a
quilter; instead, I concentrate
on the concept, color, and
design of a piece rather than
the traditional technique of
assemblage. Producing quilts is
a natural outlet for exploiting
the possibilities of cloth and
for providing a dialogue with
the viewer.

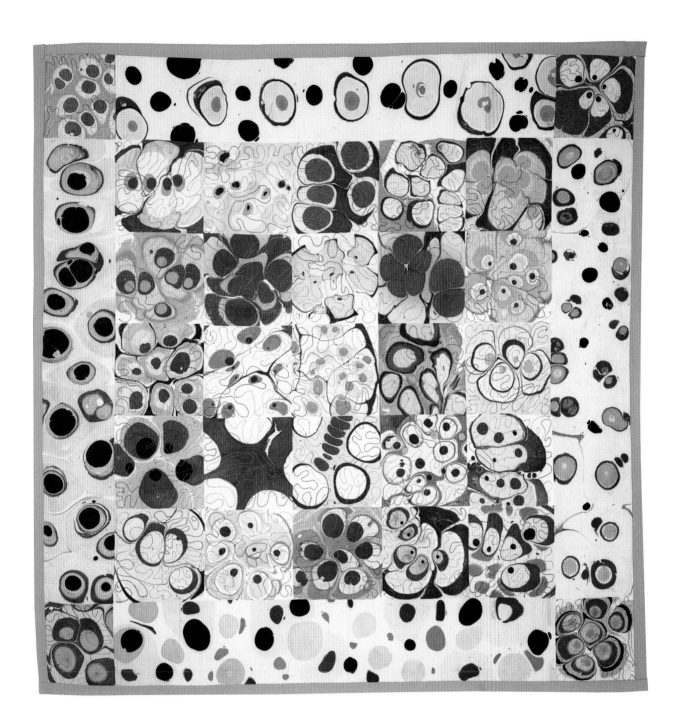

Suzanne MacGuineas
San Diego, California

Lullaby for Luke
Hand-marbled cotton fabrics created by artist; machine pieced, embroidered, and quilted; 41 x 42 inches (104 x 107 cm).

The process of creating the fabric is pure childlike joy. I have only partial control on the outcome of the design when I work with this variation on marbling. I must work very quickly and be ready for the exact moment when I let the fabric make contact with paint that is floating on a thickened liquid support. I try not to think too much, but, rather, to just keep moving in a very spontaneous way.

Jane Lloyd
Ballymena, Northern Ireland,
United Kingdom

Clockwise Circulation
Indian cotton layered and
worked in squares;
machined stitched; 54 x
35 inches (137 x 89 cm).

This is one of a series of
spiral quilts. I am interested in the play of col-
ors, and as the spirals are
quite thin, the color
blends together. Colored
stitching adds another
textured layer, while the
fraying fabric creates
more texture.

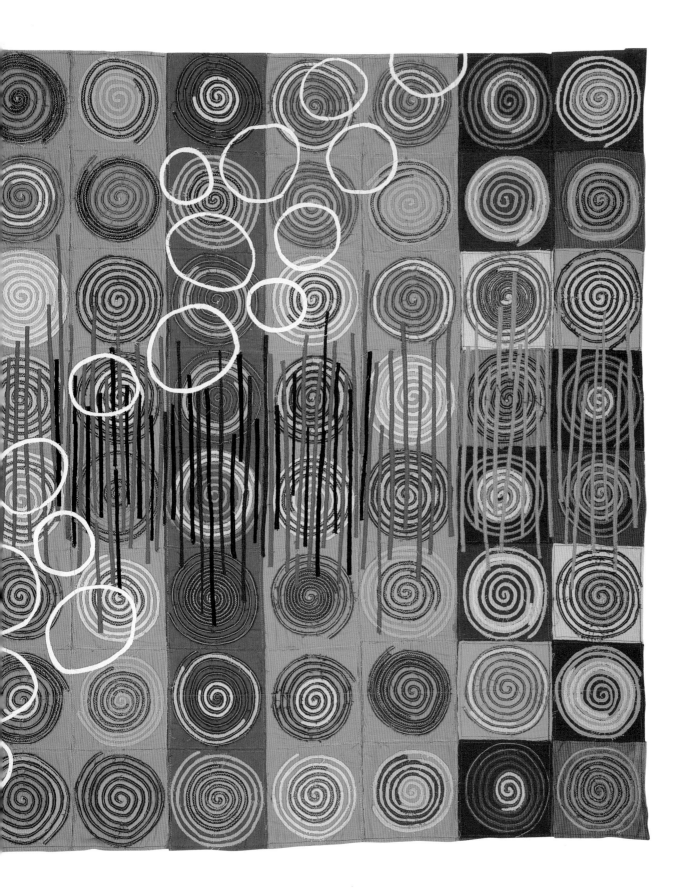

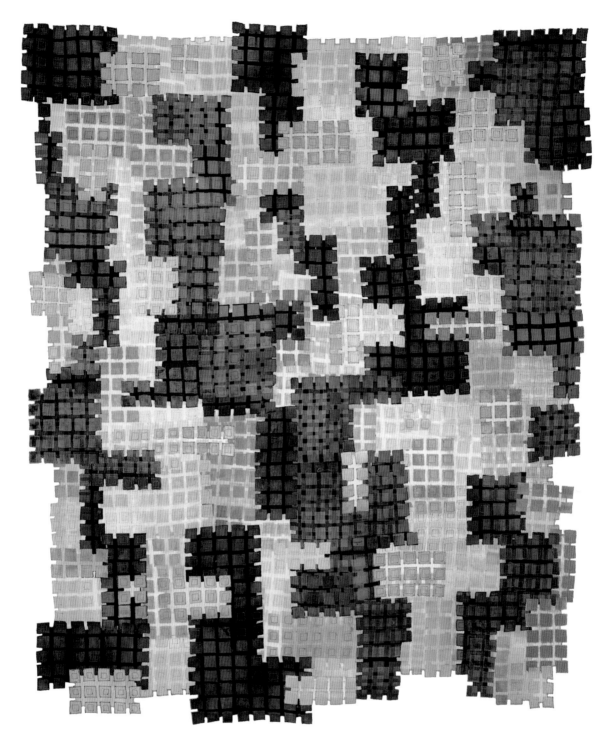

A single square unit is the fundamental element of this grid design. The individual units have formed aggregates of varying sizes, shapes, and contrasting colors, creating depth and a sense of movement. The illusion of jigsaw puzzle pieces floating on top of one another and the irregular edge of the design imply that this is a work in progress, with other pieces yet to be joined.

Judy Langille
Oak Park, Illinois

Large Puzzle Grid
Fused 100 percent cotton fabrics; painted with dyes and printed with thermofax screens; machine quilted; 49 x 59 inches (124 x 150 cm).

Maggie Bates
Anchorage, Alaska

Seeds and Pods
Ccommercial and hand- dyed cottons, paint, metal and glass beads; machine appliquéd and quilted; 28 x 44 inches (71 x 112 cm).

This quilt is my reaction to observing the incredible logic and beauty of the natural world. I did not design the seeds and pods that I interpreted in cloth, but I was amazed by the natural design in these items. For me, art is my way of acknowledging that I have taken notice of something and find it interesting enough to ask someone else to take notice as well.

I believe that my work bridges the gap between traditional needle textile arts and painting. Working with thread and fabric solves my need to create works that are beautiful, contemplative, and artistically compelling. I want to make my art inclusive, exciting, pleasurable, and substantial in content. I wish to keep traditional techniques alive by reinventing their context, promoting the value of the process while engaging in strong image making.

Bette Uscott-Woolsey
Bala Cynwyd, Pennsylvania

Quilted II
Hand-dyed painted silk; machine pieced, fused, embroidered, and hand quilted; 53 x 55 inches (135 x 140 cm).

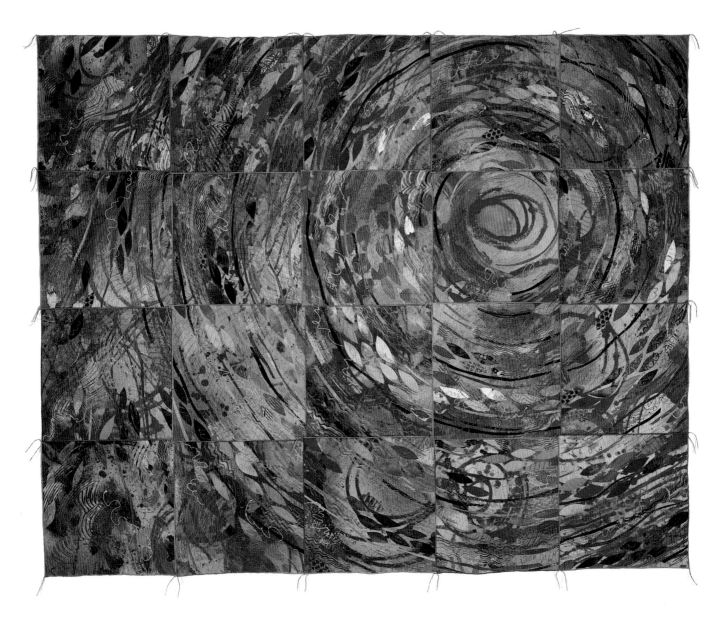

Sue Benner
Dallas, Texas

Nest III
Dye and paint on silk,
mono-printed, fused;
machine quilted, pieced
construction; 77 x 62
inches (196 x 157 cm).

Over the past twelve years I have periodically
approached the subject of motherhood in my
work. Last winter my two sons found a nest that
had fallen from a tree in our yard. I put the nest
in my studio and soon my quilts became nests. I
see an image of home and center in this series
but others see hurricanes and galaxies. I like that.

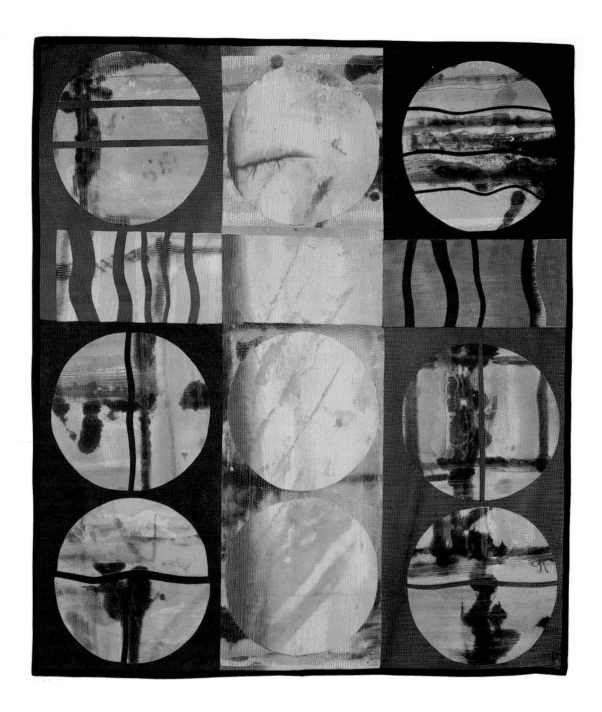

After moving from Colorado to Indiana, I noticed that the rising moon seemed much larger and the play of the clouds made interesting patterns. I did a series of "lunar" pieces from this observation. Through manipulation of the color and images and working with the positive and negative relationships, the moons and surrounding elements fell into place.

Bob Adams
Lafayette, Indiana

Lunar No. 2
100% cotton dye painted; pieced and rough-edged appliquéd, machine stitched; 32 x 36 inches (81 x 91 cm).

Patricia Malarcher
Englewood, New Jersey

Crossing
Linen fabric and primed canvas embellished with polyester film, paint, gold leaf, appliqué, and screenprinting; machine and hand stitched; 30 x 53 inches (76 x 135 cm).

My work is inspired by the use of textiles in ritual and celebration, either as architectural embellishment, vesture, or ceremonial accessories. Geometric patterning, pieced construction, collage, and appliquéd polyester film provide a means of solving formal problems as well as an expressive vocabulary.

Juror's Award of Merit

The concept of imagery from the natural world comes in part from a quote from Henry David Thoreau who said, "From the forests and wilderness come the tonics and barks which brace humankind."

Rachel Brumer
Seattle, Washington

Coral Pollen Pearls
Hand-dyed cotton, silk duppioni binding, dye sticks, textile paint, French knots, rubbed, silk screened; machine pieced, hand appliquéd, embroidered, and hand quilted; 60 x 60 inches (152 x 152 cm).

Valerie Goodwin
Tallahassee, Florida

Riverside Settlement
Cotton, silk, and blend materials; machine pieced, direct appliquéd, and fused; 35 x 49 inches (89 x 124 cm).

Quilting as a means of creative expression comes directly to me through my grandmother. As an architect, I combine this heritage with a profound need to find common ground between architectural language and the visual nature of quilting. My work uses a palette of architectural elements and principles such as figure ground relationships, the grid, built form, density, and scale. *Riverside Settlement* recalls an ancient network of interior and exterior places along a river's edge.

Lisa Call
Parker, Colorado

Structures #11
Cotton fabric hand dyed by the artist, cotton batting, cotton thread; machine pieced and quilted; 72 x 47 inches (183 x 119 cm).

This quilt is one in a series about stone walls and fences. I am intrigued by the form, lines, and shapes of these structures. In this work, I was looking to capture the beauty of the irregular spaces found between the stones in such walls. The colors of my quilts come either from my imagination or from nature. This quilt is a combination of spring colors that were particularly appealing to me on a cold winter day.

I try to work spontaneously and quickly, letting the materials and the process take over. Just as the title *Free For All* suggests, I was hoping for the spirit of light and playfulness to come bursting forth. This quilt is a celebration of life and joy.

Pat Kroth
Verona, Wisconsin

Free For All
Hand-dyed and commercial fabrics embellished with a variety of found objects (candy wrappers, paper clips, buttons, rickrack, cording, computer paper, trapped threads, stamps); fused and machine appliquéd, then machine quilted; 24 x 30 inches (61 x 76 cm).

Cher Cartwright
White Rock, British Columbia,
Canada

Rock, Paper, Scissors
Cotton fabrics hand dyed by the
artist; machine pieced and quilted;
44 x 35 inches (112 x 89 cm).

In our lives today of mass media and instant communication, there is tremendous emphasis on being attuned to what is currently considered trendy and sophisticated. Making quilts allows me to escape those concerns and tap into the part of my personality that is usually buried, and to rejoice in timeless pleasures such as simple shapes, bright colors, and children's games.

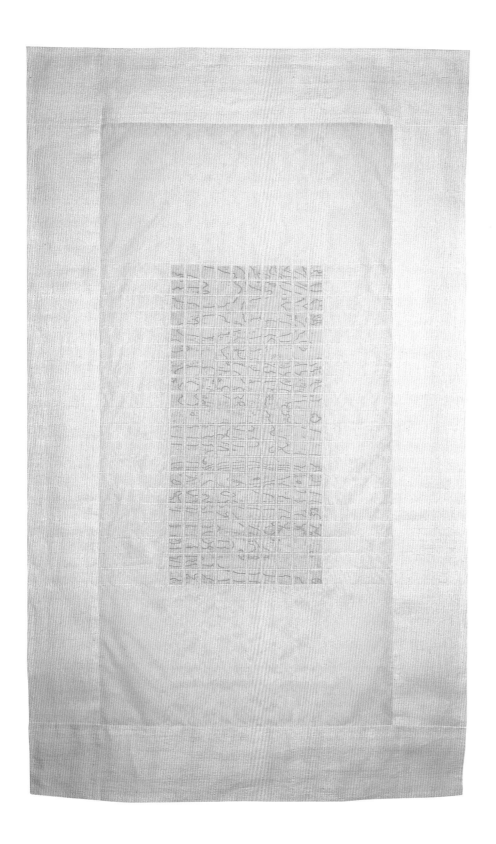

Kyoung Ae Cho
Milwaukee, Wisconsin

Veil III
Thin layer of wood (maple veneer) cut and marked with burns, sandwiched between two layers of silk organza; secured by hand stitches; 36 x 60 inches (91 x 152 cm).

Iris Aycock
Woodville, Alabama

Cedar Rose
Cotton fabric treated with
natural plant dyes and leaves;
machine quilted;
50 x 50 inches (127 x 127 cm).

This leaf hammering work is my version of an old Cherokee craft.
I find leaf forms endlessly fascinating; sometimes the imperfect
ones are more interesting than the unblemished specimens.
Occasionally I enjoy presenting them in a somewhat traditional
setting, paying homage to the quilters of past years who appliquéd
fabric leaves on their quilts.

I am now working with the form of the mountain as a part natural, part man-made construct. Human imprints such as roads, dams, mines, 'nature parks,' etc., result in a mutated tragic entity, modified to fit our needs and desires. In this image, an unknown hand has constructed a 'mountain' for its home from the detritus of the construction site.

Denise Burge
Cincinnati, Ohio

Maquette
Cotton and synthetic commercial fabrics (some hand dyed); pieced, appliqued, embroidered; 80 x 75 inches (203 x 191 cm).

Anne Woringer
Paris, France

Lucarne
Nineteenth-century linen and hemp hand spun, hand woven, and dyed by the artist; pleated and machine stitched; 45 x 62 inches (114 x 157 cm).

This quilt is from a series that visualizes log cabins made of old damaged boards. Since my country house is in a great forest, I have always been fascinated by the old trees: their trunks, roots, branches, twigs, the wood's veins, the bark, and even the logs. I also have a great fondness for primitive wood sculptures when they tend to abstraction.

Noriko Endo
Narashino, Chiba, Japan

Autumn Walk
Commercial and hand-dyed cotton, rayon, and nylon cut in small pieces and covered with soft tulle; machine quilted; 90 x 48 inches (229 x 122 cm).

This piece is part of a recent series of work that deals with landscapes. I am totally absorbed and fascinated by the beauty of nature's colors. The inspiration for this work was a series of beautiful trees with changing colors along a sidewalk in Tokyo.

I make art quilts that are portraits. Exaggerations and distortions reveal complex emotions and motivations. A secondary stitched portrait appears. Unexpected relationships of lines and shapes produce unplanned complexity, creating additional levels of interest. These double portraits symbolize lives not lived, careers not followed, lovers not married, children not born. Ambiguity, mystery, and a sense of having a life of its own are goals for work in the *Big Head Series.*

Kristin Tweed
North Fort Myers, Florida

#9 Big Head Series - The Rose
Whole cloth quilt made from recycled cotton bed sheets; machine stitched and hand painted; 42 x 45 inches (107 x 114 cm).

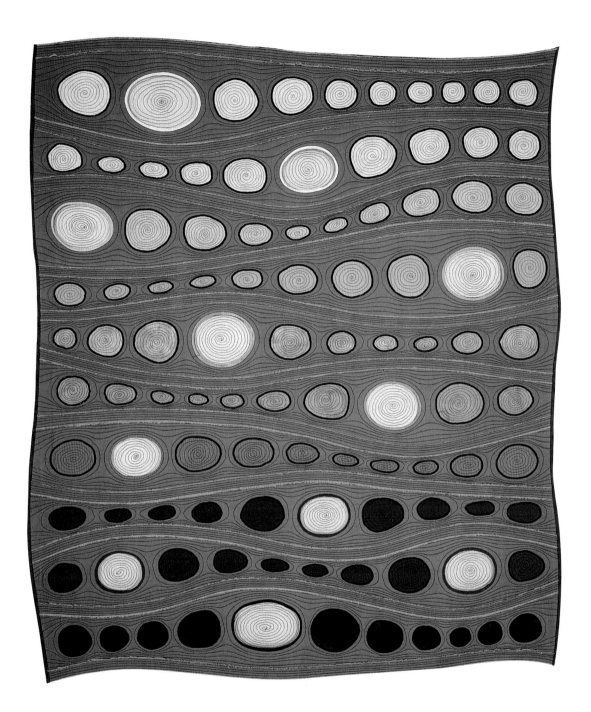

Dianne Firth
Turner, Australian Capital Territory,
Australia

One Hundred Stones
Commercial cottons, nylon
netting, polyester batting;
machine pieced, appliquéd,
and quilted; 38 x 43 inches
(97 x 109 cm).

Using the idea of placing stones to mark the passing of time, circular shapes (stones) are arranged in this quilt in ten rows of ten to represent Australia's hundred years of federation under the British monarchy in 2001. The transparent stones represent each decade's home for a republic, and the gradation of color represents the fading memory. There are actually 101 stones on the quilt, with the bottom line acknowledging the extra year taken for negotiations in 1900.

Chair is an illustration of the perfect sitting place in the ideal room, where the sitter is enthralled with pattern and thrilled by color. Dig a little deeper, and *Chair* becomes a rowdy portrait of a sacred vessel, where metaphor is understood and, ultimately, invented.

Darcy Falk
Flagstaff, Arizona

Chair (Divine Vessel Series)
Commercial, hand-dyed, and photocopied cotton, silk, polyester, and rayon fabrics; layered, fused, and stitched; 15 x 18 inches (38 x 46 cm).

Emily Richardson
Philadelphia, Pennsylvania

Full Fathom Five
Acrylic paint on linen, silk, and
cotton; hand stitched and quilted; 31
x 61 inches (79 x 155 cm). On loan
from a private collection.

Ariel sings

Full fathom five thy father lies,
Of his bones are coral made;
Those are pearls that were his eyes;
Nothing of him that doth fade,
But doth suffer a sea-change
Into something rich and strange.

From *The Tempest*, Act I, Scene 2,
by William Shakespeare

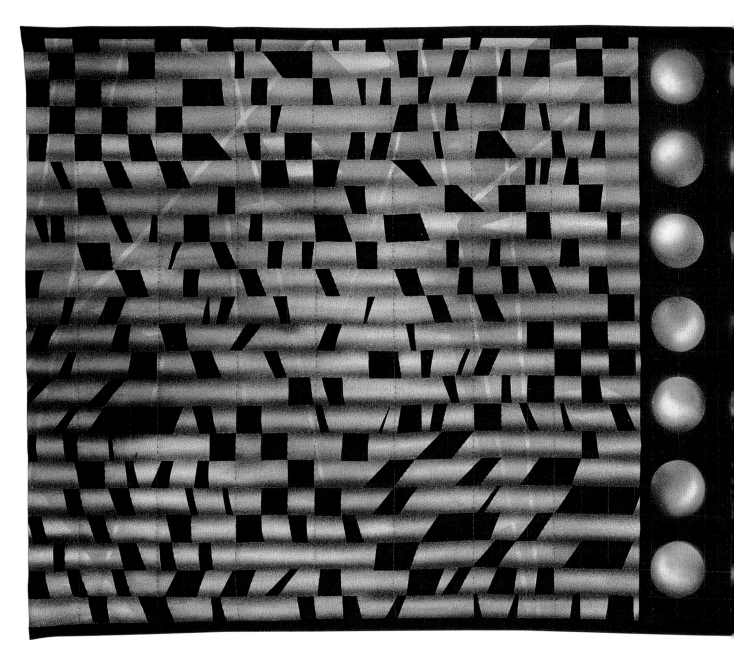

Quilts Japan Prize
Sponsored by Quilts Japan *Magazine*

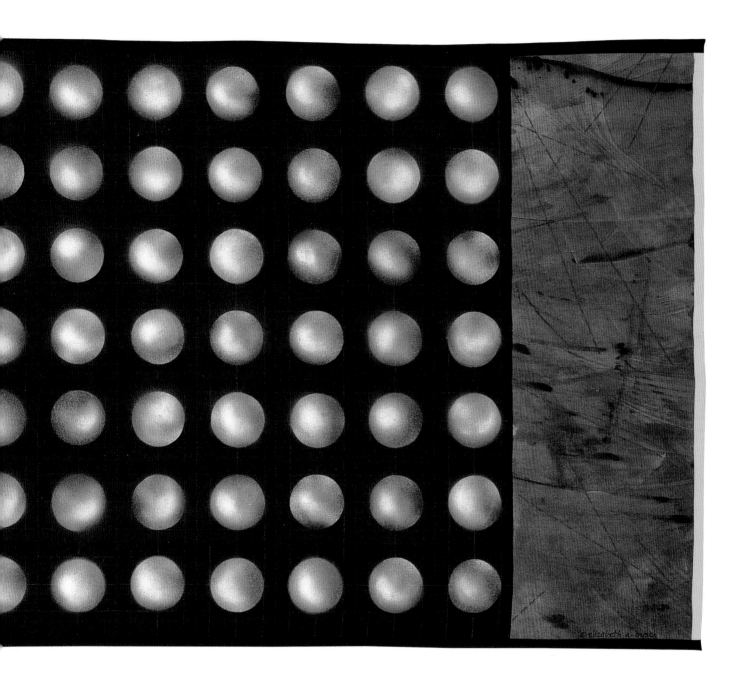

Elizabeth A. Busch
Glenburn, Maine

Abundance
Cotton canvas, purchased fabric, acrylic paint,
textile paint, hand painted, airbrushed;
machine pieced, hand and machine quilted;
54 x 22 inches (137 x 56 cm).

Abundance. I cannot keep what I don't give away.
Annie Dillard in *The Writing Life* says it all: "These
things fill from behind, from beneath, like well water. . .
Anything you do not give freely and abundantly becomes
lost to you. You open your safe and find ashes."

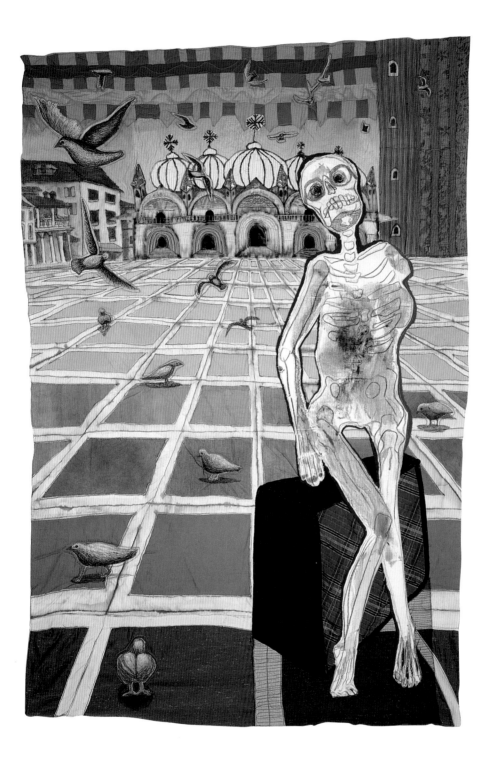

Annemarie Zwack
Ithaca, New York

Artist's First Trip to Venice
Printed commercial fabrics
hand dyed with Procion MX
dyes and embellished with an
acrylic body print (mine);
reverse appliquéd and
piecework; 51 x 78 inches
(130 x 198 cm).

This is an X-ray snapshot of
me at a turning point in my
life. You can see 'me' right
down to the bones. The birds
taking flight represent the
soaring feeling in my heart of
standing in the same piazza
where so many artists had
tread before me. I used a
body print to show the ghost
or afterimage of what the
skeleton once was.

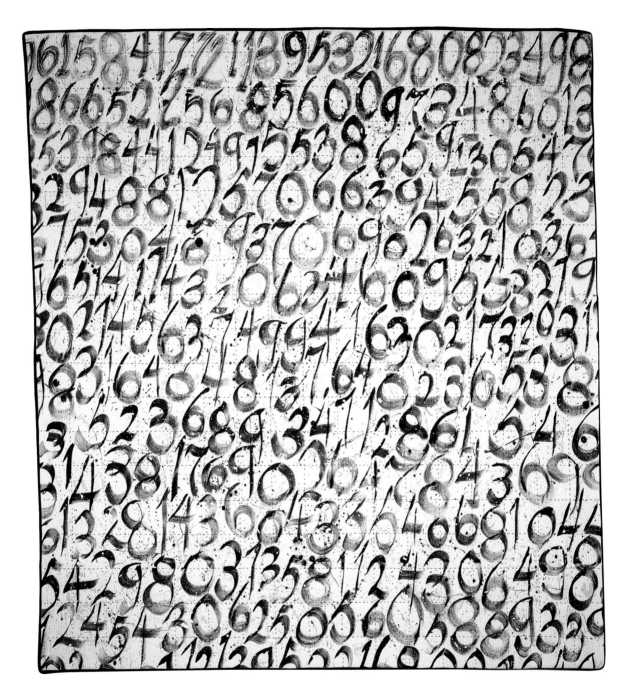

Sharon Bell
Shaker Heights, Ohio

Numbers
Whole cloth cotton twill face
and commercial cloth overdyed
by artist, sumi ink and acrylic
paints; hand quilted;
50 x 55 inches (127 x 140 cm).

This is one of a series of seven quilts visually interpreting biblical titles. Each is a whole cloth quilt that uses a dichotomy of controlled quilting techniques: the much freer application of paint or ink, the mix of traditional and contemporary, and, for this quilt, the orderliness of the mathematical universe and the randomness of numbers. The visual symbol of the *Book of Numbers* was obvious; the challenge was to make it engaging.

The cactus' rigidly patterned surface with its ribs, wrinkles, warts, hair, and thorns lies at the center of my interest. The specific colors of these gray-green plants — with their flashing orange-, pink-, and magenta-colored flowers — fascinate me. My feelings, thoughts, and memories influence the creative process so that the piece does not simply reflect nature. It is my aim to bring rhythm and color to a symbiosis.

Ursula König
Bern, Switzerland

Cactus
Commercial and hand-dyed cotton fabrics; machine pieced and quilted; 35 x 50 inches (89 x 127 cm).

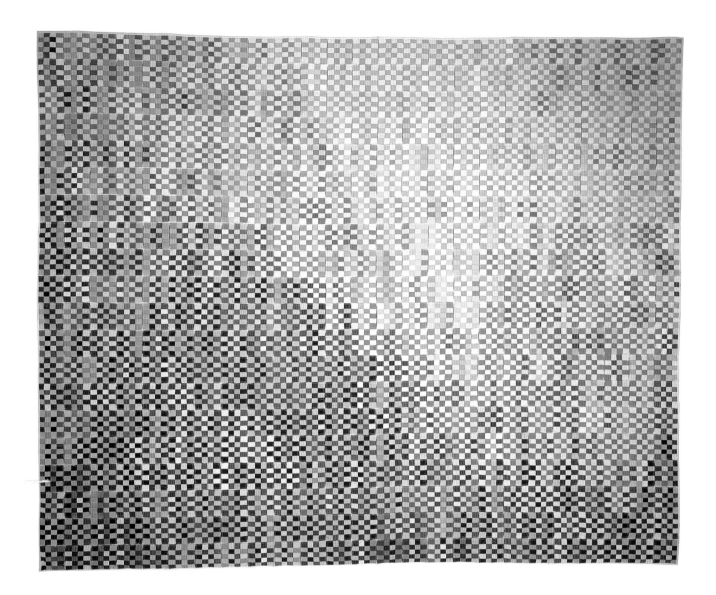

Inge Hueber
Köln, Germany

Sweet melodies of colors, played
in the summer of 2001.

Colour Melody (Summer 2001)
Home-dyed cotton; machine pieced and
quilted; 91 x 72 inches (231 x 183 cm).

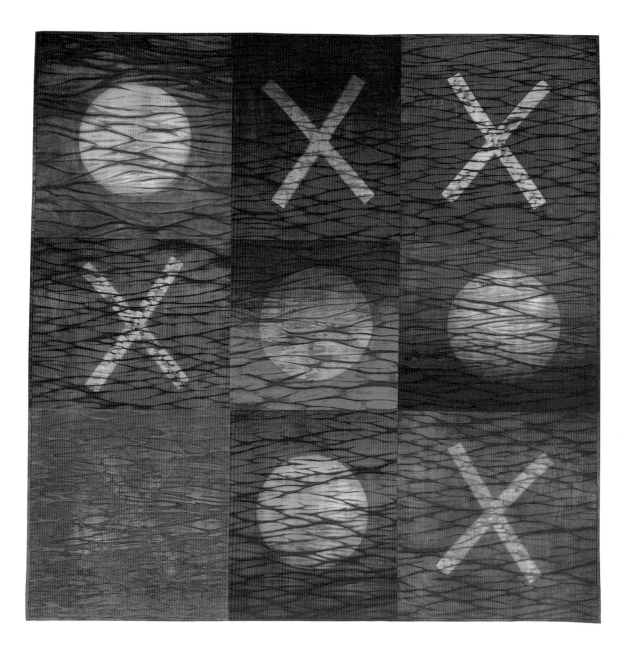

A *Cat's Game* is a conclusion in which nobody wins. I am rarely political in my work, but apparently present and proposed military engagements have "ooched" their way into the consciousness of my dye pot. My nine-year-old son offered several compositional suggestions by providing me, at my request, with an array of cat games. My first collaboration!

Jan Myers-Newbury
Pittsburgh, Pennsylvania

Cat's Game
Kona cotton, dyed by the artist using various forms of mechanical resist; machine pieced and quilted; 55 x 56 inches (140 x 142 cm).

Sushma Patel-Bould
East Palo Alto, California

Bauhaus
Cotton fabrics; machine pieced and quilted; 36 x 72 inches (91 x 183 cm).

This quilt is a tribute to our female ancestors who embraced modern production technologies to bring the beauty of hand-crafted arts to many. The natural harmonies of earth and sky contrast and balance the precise geometry of this machine-quilted textile. The bold, vibrant color juxtaposed by delicately veiled quilting lines transforms the warp and weft into a unified whole.

Juror's Award of Merit

Colorado's mountain environs and natural colors constantly inspire my fabric dyeing and design. The combination of their white bark, black scarring by elk antlers, and their unique shaking green leaves (called "Colorado gold" in the fall) makes Aspen poplar trees mesmerizing at any season. My hope is *Aspen Seasons* brings you peace and tranquility.

Patty Hawkins
Estes Park, Colorado

Aspen Seasons
Cottons with patterns created by the artist, free-cut curved and pieced to imitate tree trunk vertical shapes; 78 x 34 inches (198 x 86 cm); two-panel piece.

Transcending the impersonal objectivity of geometric abstraction through the sensuousness of materials, my works reveal a blend of reason and passion, reflecting my nature. I find inspiration in diverse sources, including the complexity of Indian miniatures, the mystery of Russian icons, the lush intensity of Matisse paintings, and the elegance of kesa robes worn by Japanese monks.

Marilyn Henrion
New York, New York

Night Thoughts # 2
Silk, cotton, and metallic fabrics; hand pieced and quilted; 51 x 53 inches (130 x 134 cm).

Joan Schulze
Sunnyvale, California

Concert Hall
Silk, cotton, and paper;
monoprinting, photocopy and glue
transfer processes, pieced, machine
stitched, and quilted; 50 x 50 inches
(127 x 127 cm). On loan from The
Oakland Museum of California.

Concert Hall is a place where people dressed in
tuxedos stand around waiting for the music to
begin. Perhaps it has already begun.

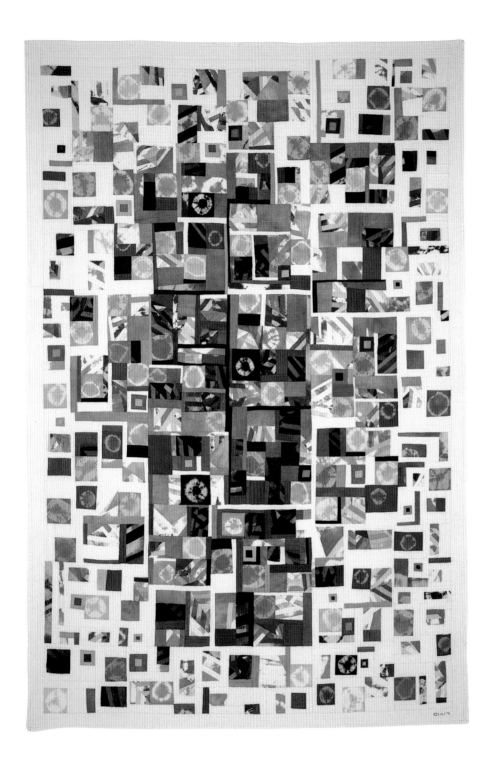

Mi Sik Kim
Nonsan City, Korea

The Years Lost
Commercial and hand-dyed
cottons; machine pieced and
hand quilted; 49 x 73 inches
(124 x 185 cm).

I feel that my memories,
both painful and joyful,
change as time passes;
sometimes they remain,
sometimes they fade
away. Memories are like
stitching and sewing:
when many small pieces
join together to make a
larger one, they transform
into something new.

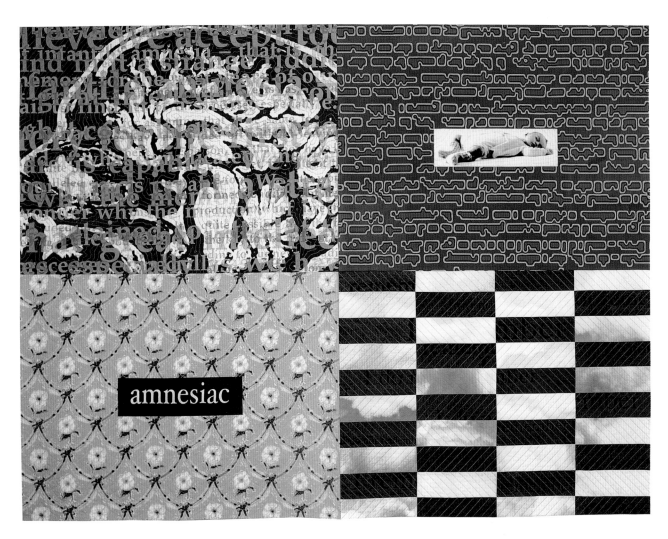

Award for Most Innovative Use of the Medium, sponsored by Friends of Fiber Art International

Michael James
Lincoln, Nebraska

A Strange Riddle
100% cotton surface embellished with digitally developed and printed images using Photoshop and CAD software and a Mimaki textile printer; machine pieced and quilted; 76 x 57 inches (193 x 145 cm).

A 1949 photograph taken by my father when I was five months old and an essay by Freud on the mystery of infantile amnesia were the triggers for this quilt. The child's neurological immaturity would seem to prevent the "reading" of visual patterns, such as the genteel floral wallpaper of that first room, but can we be sure? While I don't have any memories of that first bedroom, I am fascinated by pattern of all kinds, and believe that fascination has deeply embedded roots.

Meiny
Vermaas-van der Heide
Tempe, Arizona

Earth Quilt #106: Lines XVIII
Commercial and hand-dyed cotton fabrics
(made as a group effort in a two-day
workshop with Heide Stoll-Weber in
Germany); machine pieced and quilted;
66 x 46 inches (168 x 117 cm). Sashiko
topstitching pattern from the book *Sashiko*
by Mary S. Parker, adapted by the artist.

My quilts are known for their strong
graphics, minimalist appeal, and the
color magic of visual illusions. My trade-
mark wrinkled heirloom appearance
within the quilt surface and the crisp
edge of the binding juxtaposed with the
influence of Mondrian and the Dutch
style reveals my fascination with mid-
century modern as well as op art, making my quilts 'contemporary classics.'

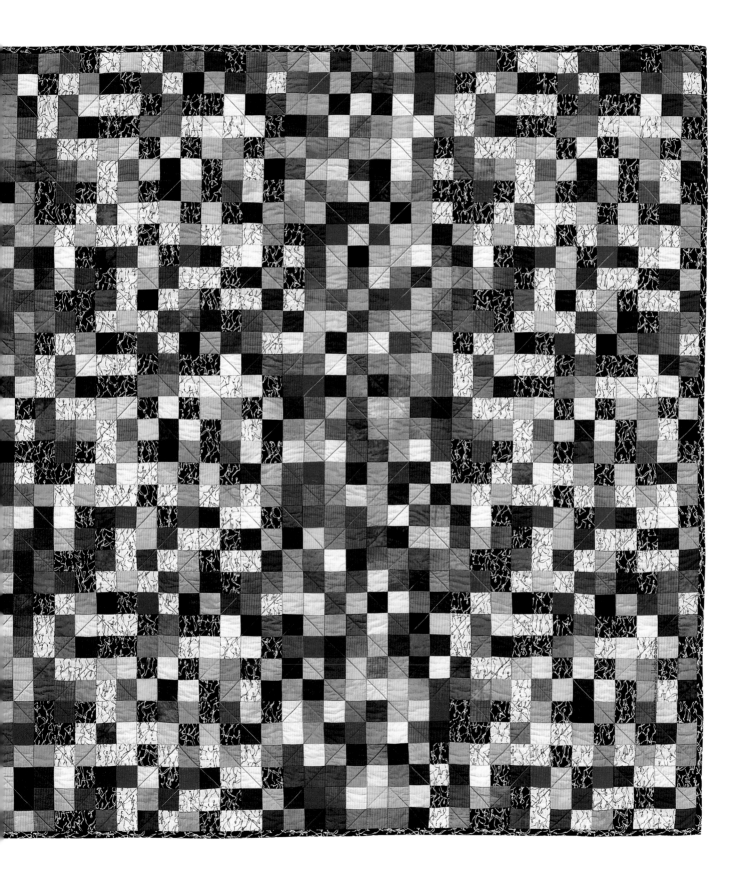

Marie L. Jensen
Tacoma, Washington

Global Warming
Raw canvas embellished with
fabric paint and photo transfers;
machine pieced and appliquéd;
25 x 40 inches (64 x 102).

Inspired by a local radio station's
ecology report, this is a somewhat light approach to a serious
concern. Just as the flood of rising waters from melting ice caps
threatens our environment, the
deluge of daily responsibilities
and information makes me feel
like I'm only treading water.

Judith Rush
Bexley, Ohio

Wheat Fields in Egypt #1
Hand-dyed cotton; machine
pieced and quilted; 31 x 33
inches (79 x 84 cm).

Artists in ancient Egypt lived in a world of fascinating and brilliant colors. I had a unique opportunity to visit Egypt, and my Egyptian companions provided extraordinary insight and guidance as we traveled many different types of sites. The overwhelming feeling of awe I felt left me with sweaty palms that ran the colors from my sketchbook. This piece is one of my efforts to communicate that feeling of trembling excitement.

Susan Shie & James Acord
Wooster, Ohio

The Dish Soap/Hermit:
Card #9 in the Kitchen Tarot
Recycled bridal train and dish towels, cotton and satin fabrics, assorted trims, shrink art drawings, shisha mirrors; appliquéd, airbrushed, hand painted, hand quilted and embroidered; 34 x 59 inches (86 x 150 cm).

The dish soap bottle sits under the sink in the dark cupboard, like a hermit. The lace appliqué pattern down the middle of the bridal train found by Lucky (Susan) suggested the form of the dish soap bottle, so off we went to Card #9 out of 78 Kitchen Tarot cards!!!! Lucky wrote lots of little diary stories while slowly stitching: "Finding the Carnival Glass Butterdish with Pat," "Sharing the Diamond Ring with Gretchen," and "Getting Hattie's Knee Operation."

Margery Goodall
Mount Lawley, Western Australia,
Australia

Summer: Harvest #2
Cotton, cotton blend, lamé blend, and
rayon fabrics; machine pieced and
quilted; 19 x 30 inches (48 x 76 cm).

The organic qualities of a hand-
stitched line sewn with a single
thread are represented by machine
stitched segments of machine
woven fabric, and make reference
to the colors and lines of a wheat
field. Australian farmers have been
called the best in the world, but
farming is tough in this country,
and each year when our farmers
sow a crop in this drought-prone
environment, they take a leap of
faith. I salute their dreams and
their courage with this quilt.

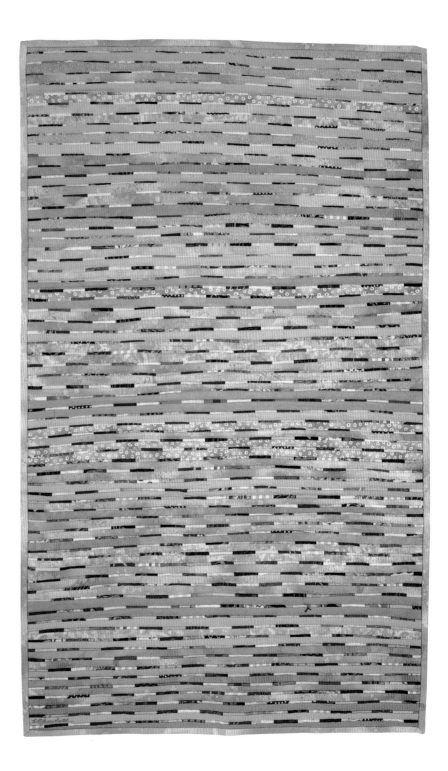

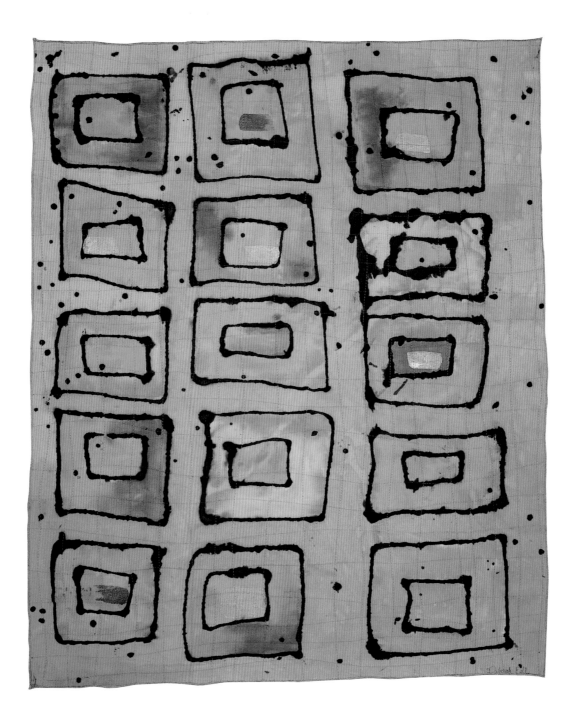

This quilt is the third in the series of the *Tuesday's Child/Rebuilding* pieces. Continuing with the theme of destruction and rebuilding, this piece is very simple. Much of the country believes they have been changed because of the September 11, 2001, terrorist events, and I am no exception. My previous work was somewhat representational, but things are not so clear to me now and my work reflects this in a more abstract form.

Deborah Fell
Urbana, Illinois

Painted Squares
Whole cloth quilt, dye-painted and stamped by artist; machine quilted; 35 x 42 inches (89 x 107).

Ellin Larimer
Nordland, Washington

Verdant Counterpoint
Hand-dyed (by the artist) pima
and kona cottons and several
commercially dyed cottons;
machine pieced and quilted;
54 x 70 inches (137 x 178 cm).

I am inspired by our northwest woods and ground covers
and have tried to express that feeling with curved lines and
shapes. *Counterpoint* seemed an appropriate title because I
was combining the motifs into a single harmonic texture. I
wanted a rhythmic quality in my work, and my quilting
continued this feeling.

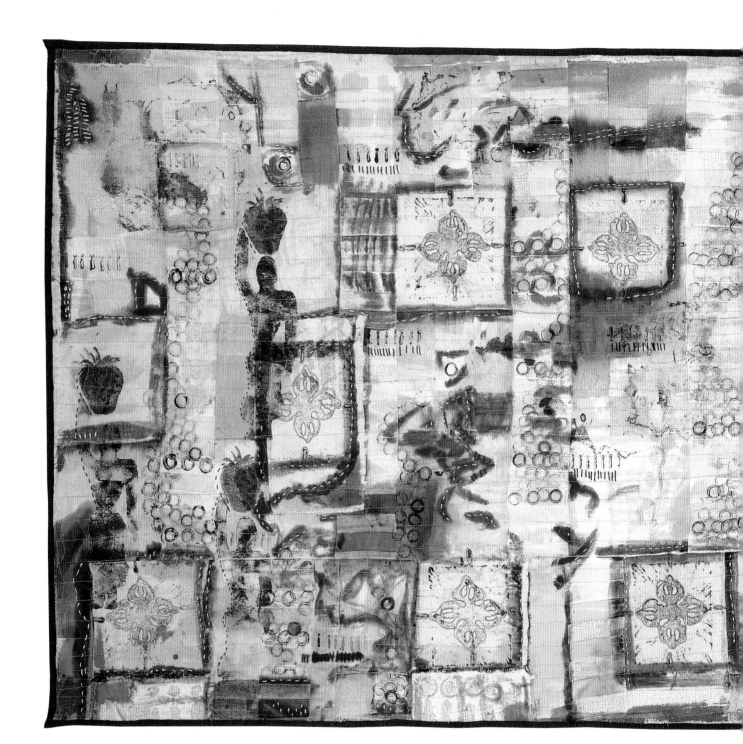

Marylouise Learned
Boulder, Colorado

Sign and Symbol
Pieced cotton, silk, gauze, and canvas; dye painted, monoprinted, stamped, hand stitched, machine and free-motion quilted; 62 x 33 inches (157 x 84 cm).

There is always some connection to the traditional arts, done primarily by women, in my work. It is my link to history, to my ancestors, and to the feminine principles of nurture, nature, and enjoyment. Each piece is a birth of some sort. Whether its duration is long or short, there comes a time to say good-bye and clear the decks for the next arrival. My visual day-to-day life and music serve as metaphors for this process.

This is the first of three works using ocean life as a subject. The lion fish inspired me with its color variations, tentacle shapes, and delicate movements. The fish became the dominant subject, with various layers of textures as the background.

Leslie Gabriëlse
Rotterdam, The Netherlands

Lion Fish
Various fabrics, hand appliquéd with yarn and thread, embellished with acrylic paint; 86 x 68 inches
218 x 173 cm).

Patricia Autenrieth
Hyattsville, Maryland

Picnic
Cotton, blends, linen; screen
printing, hand appliqué, English
paper piecing, machine quilting;
49 x 52 inches (124 x 132 cm).

Everyday forms and materials, autobiographical
elements, art historical references, and traditional
quilting designs always seem to collide in my
work. I sometimes feel that I act as artistic valet,
looking for places for all these things to park.

Juror's Award of Merit

Dinah Sargeant
Newhall, California

Link
100% cotton fabric hand painted by
the artist; hand and machine
appliquéd, machine-pieced
background, hand and machine
quilted; 84 x 78 inches
(213 x 198 cm).

One night two owls flew overhead. Oblivious to me, they clicked and glided together in their own world. I walked in mine, feeling privileged for the glimpse of theirs, and then, recognized our connection.

Judith Content
Palo Alto, California

Desert Pools
100% black Thai silk that has been pleated, discharged, and Arashi shibori dyed; machine quilted and pieced; 68 x 67 inches (173 x 170 cm).

Desert pools are evolutionary wonders of time and isolation — temporary vessels of ancient soil filled by winter rains, each tiny refuge cradling plant and animal life uniquely its own. A sanctuary for aquatic plants and animals, wildflowers, and migratory birds, desert pools are a source of life extending far into the surrounding landscape. This piece was inspired by the ephemeral beauty of these miniature oases and celebrates their preservation.

Nest IX: Generations continues my Nest series that was initiated when my daughter left home for college. With the September 11 bombings, the concept of "home" as expressed through the metaphor "nest" became much more significant and global. This series calls attention to temporality, resiliency, growth, the combination of fragility and strength, and, in this piece especially, family relationships and what gets passed along.

Erika Carter
Bellevue, Washington

Nest IX: Generations
Discharged cotton (bleach, stopped with anti-chlor); machine pieced and quilted; 38 x 48 inches (97 x 122 cm).

Linda Levin
Wayland, Massachusetts

Central Park West / Winter I
Cotton and other fabrics, Procion
dyed; machine stitched; 44 x 55
inches (112 x 140 cm).

My quilts are made with fabrics I dye myself to
achieve a spontaneity purchased fabrics don't
provide. I try to capture not a specific scene, but
an atmosphere, a mood or a moment.

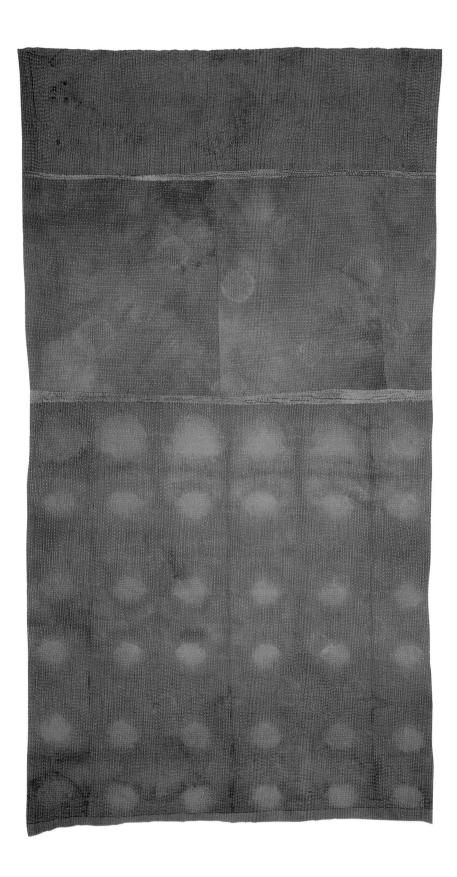

Pamela Fitzsimmons
Mount Vincent, New South Wales, Australia

Fossil Bed #2
Wool and silk, dyed with eucalyptus leaves; machine pieced, hand stitched with silk thread; 29 x 52 inches (74 x 132 cm).

Time imprinted on an ancient dry landscape, shaped by wind and water . . . layers of fossils revealing fragments of life long past . . . fabric folded, scrunched, and stained with leaves and bark . . . repetitive hand stitches conveying a sense of time and labor. . .

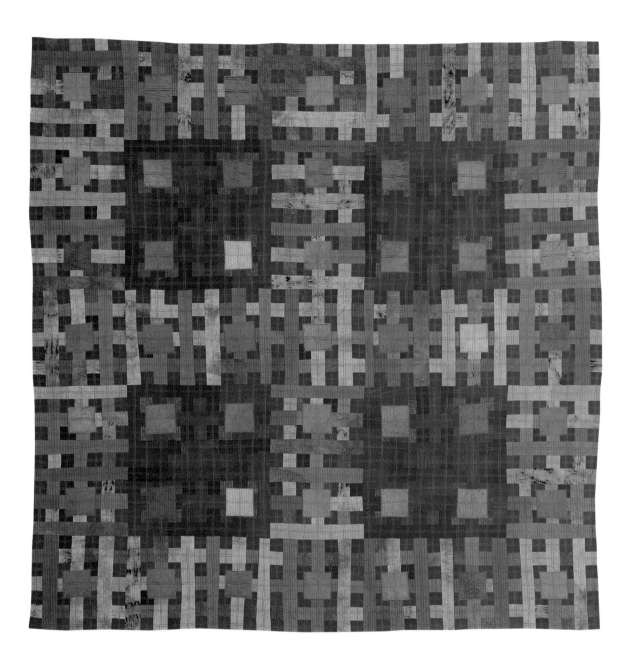

Eleanor A. McCain
Shalimar, Florida

Crab
Hand-dyed cotton fabric (by the artist and
others); machine pieced and quilted;
90 x 90 inches (229 x 229 cm).

Quilting is grounded in American history, family, community, and common experience. Art quilts are a living docu-
ment of cultural history, expressing artistic, emotional,
and spiritual values, particularly those of women. I use
quilts to transpose function and symbol, art and craft, and
to express ideas about creativity and community.
Crab uses the colors found on the shell of the female
Florida blue brab, *Callinectes sapidus.* The grid structure is a
format for exploration of color and spatial relationships.

Barbara W. Watler
Hollywood, Florida

Spiral Leaf
Cotton fabric; machine satin
stitched and reverse appliquéd; 69
x 38 inches (175 x 97 cm).

Leaves, like fingerprints, have "one-of-a-kind" designs. The organic labyrinth created by this coleus leaf is a spiral pathway, leading the eye on a spiritual journey through islands of black and white to an inner destination.

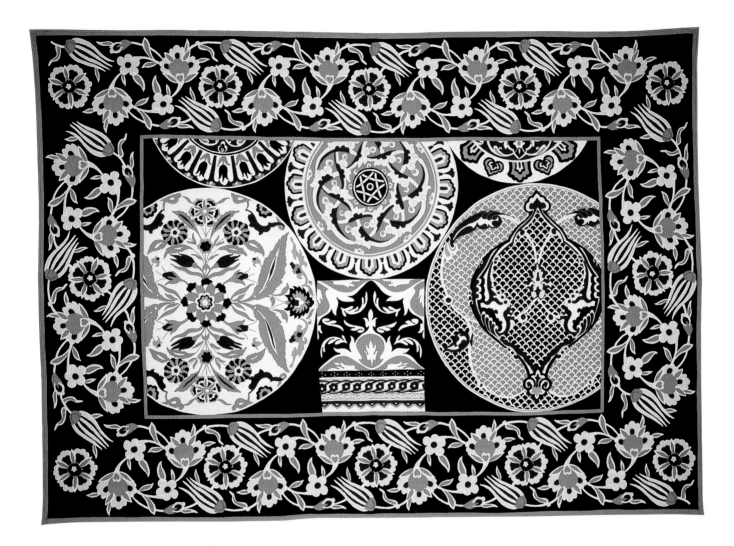

I finish every detail of my work completely by hand sewing, using a traditional technique, as I respect heritage and tradition. I love handwork, and would like to devote as much of my time as possible to making quilts.

Hiromi Hayashi
Nagasaki, Japan

Arabesque Plates
Cotton fabrics; pieced, appliquéd, embroidered, and quilted by hand; 102 x 72 inches (259 x 183 cm).

Linda MacDonald
Willits, California

Wildlife Sanctuaries
Cotton broadcloth, airbrushed,
hand painted; hand quilted; 45 x
34 inches (114 x 86 cm).

Northern California is converting its forest land to vine-
yards, suburbs, and plush vacation retreats. These
changes affect the wildlife to a large, usually negative
degree. There is hope, though: migration routes from
one shrinking habitat to another and underpasses for
roads and freeways are being considered in state highway
and development plans. In the worst sense, the animals
in this piece show how small their natural habitats may
become by having only a small sanctuary to live in.

Award of Excellence

What once was hot
Eventually gets cold.
What once was full
Eventually gets empty.
It is up to you to "Recharge" it.

Ludmilla Uspenskaya
New York, New York

Recharge
Silk and cotton fabrics hand painted by artist,
wax resist, collage; machine and hand
quilted; 56 x 74 inches (142 x 188 cm).

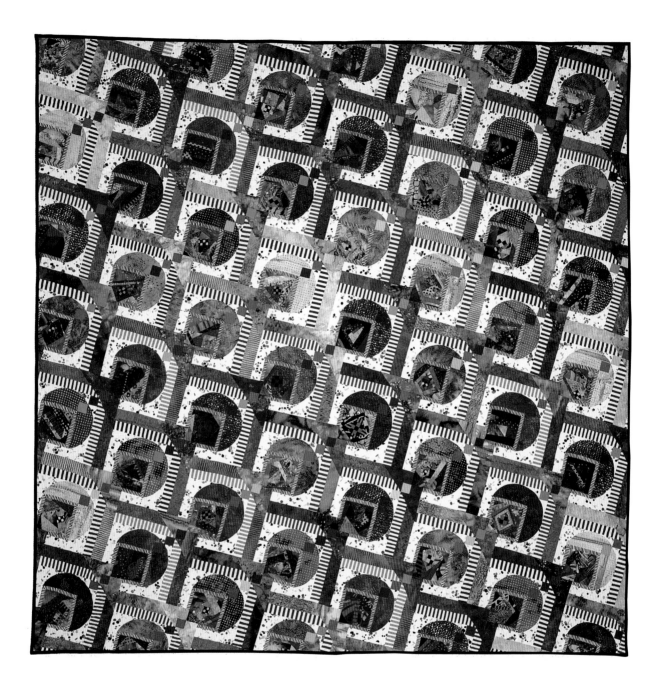

Sharon Heidingsfelder
Little Rock, Arkansas

Grab your perogies . . .
it's circus time!

Popcorn, Peanuts, and Cracker Jacks!
Cotton, commercially printed
fabric, some printed fabric by
artist; repeat block design
machine pieced and quilted;
73 x 74 inches (185 x 188 cm).

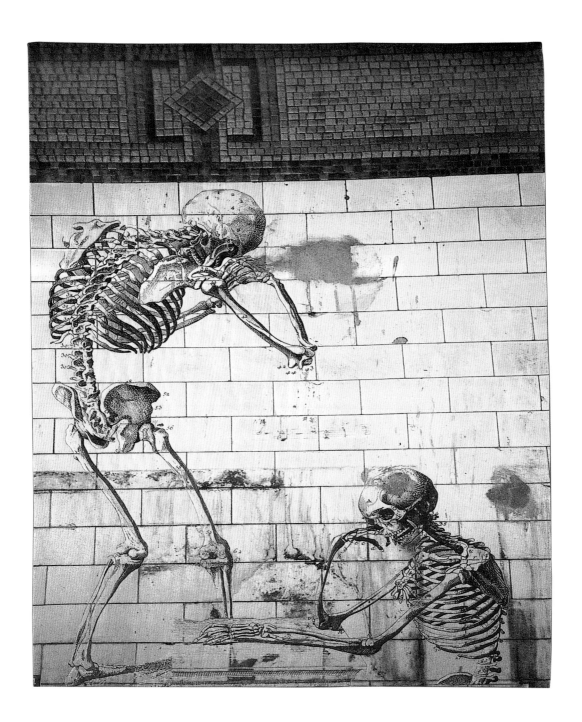

In November of 2001 I spent a week in New York and visited Ground Zero to pay my respects. In the past, I had taken the subway to the Twin Towers as a tourist destination. Now Cortland Street Station, a stop for the World Trade Center, is completely closed. As I traveled underground, I imagined that people might have been entombed at Cortland Street. Passing through the subway system, dirt and markings on station walls caught my attention.

Miriam Nathan-Roberts
Berkeley, California

Cortland Street Subway Station
Digitally designed and digitally printed on cotton sateen with fiber reactive dyes; machine quilted; 42 x 49 inches (107 x 124 cm).

Patricia Mink
Ann Arbor, Michigan

Concrete Abstraction
Inkjet pigments printed onto various fabrics
(silk, cotton, blends, disposable face cloths);
fusible appliqué, machine quilted, and
embroidered; 28 x 36 inches (71 x 91 cm).

Layers are the focus of my work in several ways: as components of physical structure, as elements of process, and as complex metaphor. *Concrete Abstraction* was created from photographic images of several different walls, collaged together. The different patterns and textures that occur in aging walls as a result of construction, deterioration, and reconstruction set up interesting visual relationships and contrasts, especially when reproduced in softer materials.

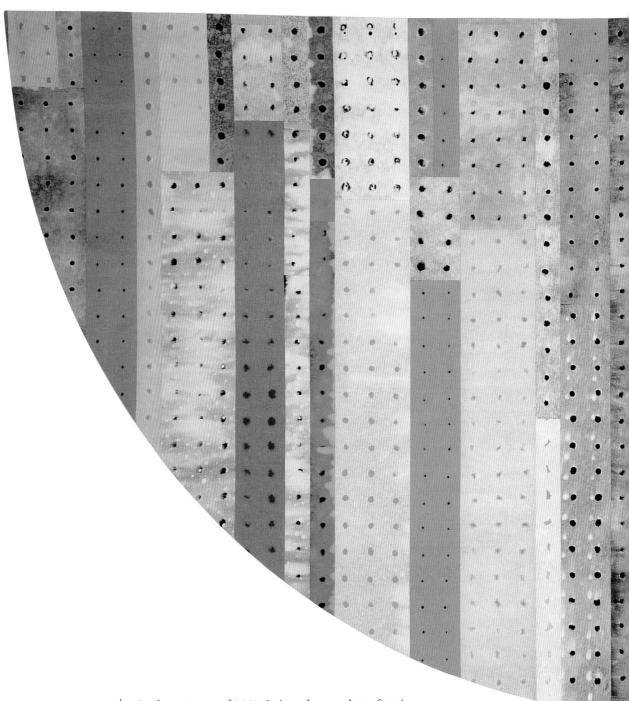

Martha Warshaw
Cincinnati, Ohio

Cope: Scattering
New and recycled fabrics;
bleached and/or inked; machine
pieced and hand tied; 107 x 54
inches (272 x 137 cm).

In the summer of 2001, I viewed a number of antique
ecclesiastical copes (capes) on display in European museums. One 14th-century cope, worn out after centuries of use,
had been cut up and used in three new vestments. In the
19th century, those three vestments were taken apart and the
original cope was reassembled. In the 20th century, what
remained of the cope was stitched to velvet for display.

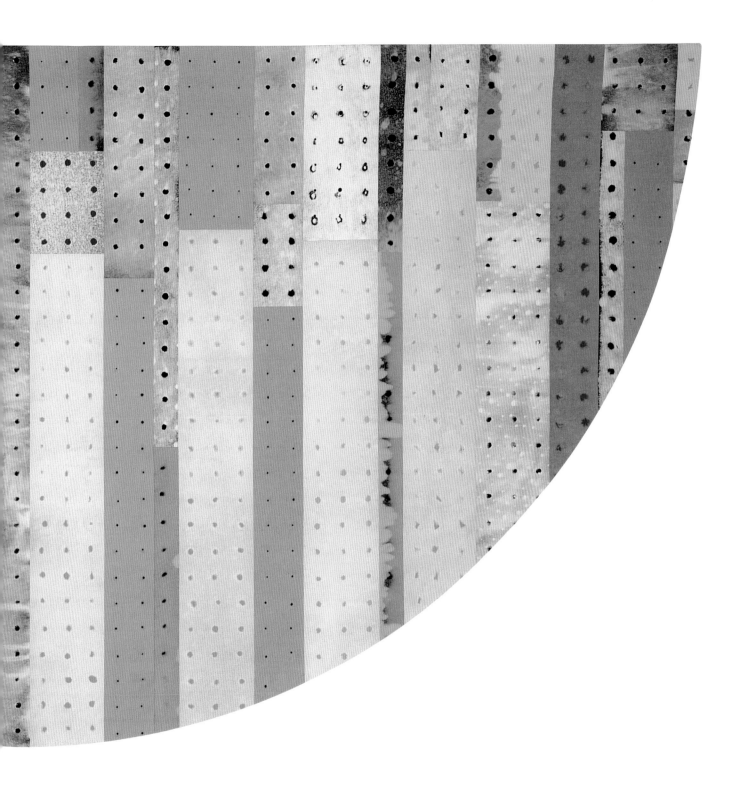

It's surprising to look at familiar objects in a new context, such as when setting up a still-life composition. Often the homeliest or most ordinary things have the most interesting shapes and patterns when abstracted and made to interact with each other. The challenge of exploring and developing these relationships into a satisfying arrangement, and then translating it into fabric on a two-dimensional plane, keeps me interested in pursuing this series.

Dominie Nash
Bethesda, Maryland

Stills from a Life 4
Cotton and silk, hand dyed, drawn, and printed by the artist; machine appliquéd and quilted; 61 x 60 inches (155 x 152 cm).

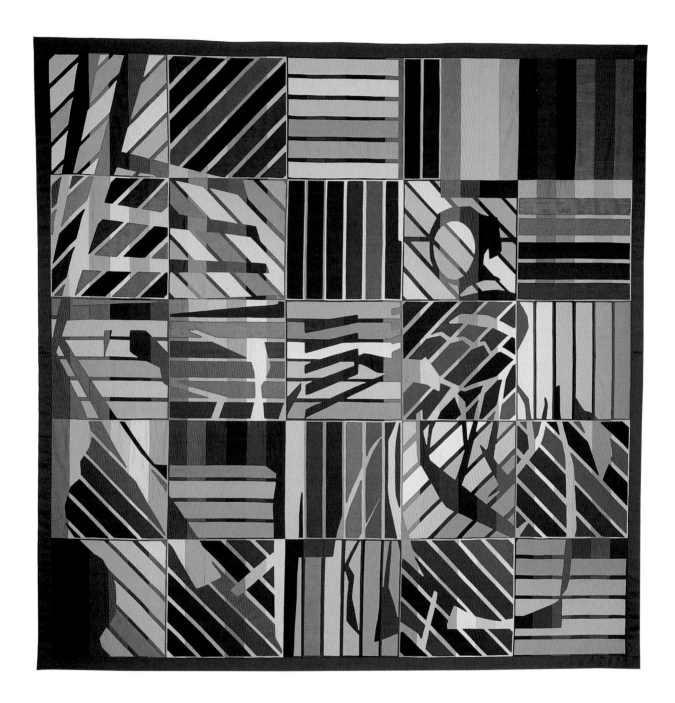

Anne McKenzie Nickolson
Indianapolis, Indiana

Woman Still Seated
Commercially dyed cotton; machine pieced, hand appliquéd through all layers; 57 x 57 inches (145 x 145 cm).

This work was inspired by Jan Vermeer's *A Lady Seated at the Virginal.* I was especially interested in the painting's structure and luminosity, which I tried to capture in my quilt. Viewing paintings is an important activity for me, and I am especially moved by the persistent power of Vermeer's paintings. It is because the 17th-century painting "still" effects me (and others) that the woman is "still seated."

On my wonder ride of everyday experiences, I race and rummage through memories of living in the South, the East Coast, and my Indiana childhood. *Good Humor* contains salvaged fragments of my husband's portrait, a photograph shot while passing an ice cream truck, and my own left hand. I record anecdotes in cryptic disarray, saturating the surface of the most intimate fabric of the home: the sheets on the bed. Tucked in, my personal history unfolds.

Jen Swearington
Asheville, North Carolina

Good Humor
Pieced bed sheets, layers of gesso, shellac; charcoal and grease pencil drawing, screen printing, free-motion embroidery, and quilting; 24 x 34 inches (61 x 81 cm).

Orna Roglit
Ramat-Hasharon, Israel

Traces III
Hand-printed and dyed
cotton (by the artist) and
multilayered torn strips;
machine pieced and
quilted; 41 x 55 inches
(104 x 140 cm).

In the beginning GOD created
The heaven that doesn't exist
And the earth willing to touch it,
Pulling strings between them.
With his tenderness touch
He created the Man-to-be
A prayer, a string, for the never exist.

"Traces" A connection between art and reality
It reflects my feelings motion and energy
At different times during life.
My printed fabrics and torn stripes in
continuously repeated
Lines, create the illusion of movement

Wildflowers reflects my love for gardening, working with the exuberance and raw energy of flowers. Each one is different, yet together they entice you with a blast of color. I hoped to capture some of that excitement.

Carol Owen
Pittsboro, North Carolina

Wildflowers
Commercial and hand-painted cotton, torn and sewn edge strips; 45 x 42 inches (114 x 107 cm).

John w. Lefelhocz
Athens, Ohio

Match Schticks
Bonded paper and nylon net embellished with matchsticks, fabric, beads, and knotted rope, all bordered by peach skin over cotton duck; 62 x 73 inches (157 x 185 cm). Corset images provided by Ann Moneypenny of 100 Proof Press.

Striking, isn't it?

Weaving is fine, but sometimes I like to use glue . . . lots of glue. — J.w.L.

"The ritual of marriage is not simply a social event; it is a crossing of threads in the fabric of fate. Many strands bring the couple and their families together and spin their lives into a fabric that is woven on their children."
— Portuguese-Jewish Wedding Ceremony

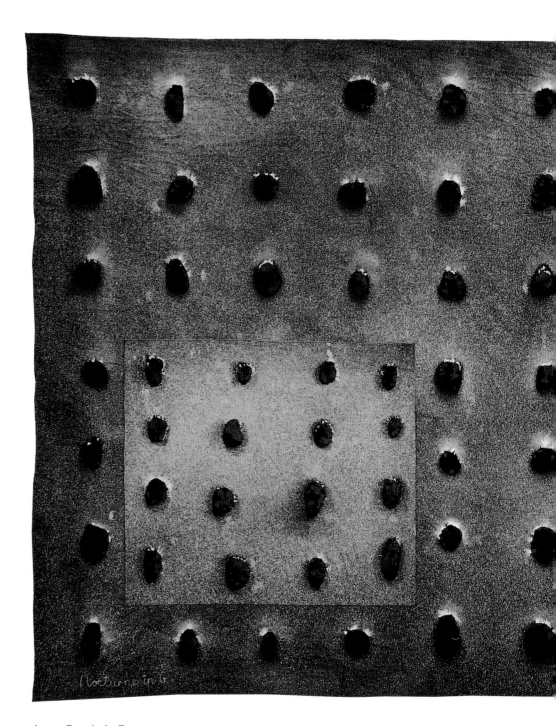

Lynn Goodwin Borgman
Memorial Award for Surface Design

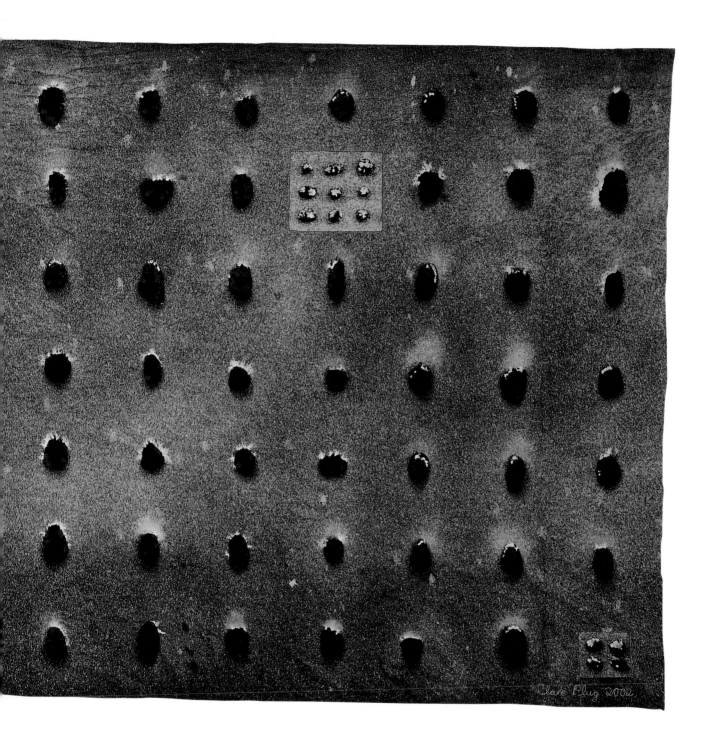

Clare Plug
Napier, New Zealand

Nocturne in G
Discharge-dyed cotton; machine quilted
and reverse appliquéd; 74 x 39 inches
(188 x 99 cm).

My current work is created in response to the coastline
where I live: the rhythms, patterns, and textures and its
emptiness and limited color schemes all excite me. The
inspiration for this particular quilt was the graywacke stones
that blanket our city beach combined with the formality of
the beachfront gardens.

I like to have my photographic images made into halftones before I print them because it alters the viewer's perception, making the line between appearance and reality a little hazier.

Sandi Cummings
Moraga, California

Ladies of the Day
Commercial, hand-dyed, and screen-printed cottons and blends; machine pieced and quilted; 74 x 66 inches (188 x 168 cm).

Kathleen Loomis
Louisville, Kentucky

Black I
Selvages from commercial and hand-dyed cottons; machine appliquéd and quilted in one step; 42 x 45 inches (107 x 114 cm).

Fabric always speaks to me, but selvages have a lot more to say than most fabrics! My father is a typographer, so type and graphic arts have been an integral part of my personal life as well as my career in journalism and corporate communication. This is one of a series of alphabet quilts focusing on single letters, executed in different techniques, but always revealing their essential form and beauty.

Vortex is a quilt about energy and movement. Here is a metaphoric whirlpool of planetary thought patterns. A powerful undercurrent scoops up almost everything in its path, but at the same time its excessive force spins off new and opposing currents of awareness.

Jane A. Sassaman
Chicago, Illinois

Vortex
Cotton fabrics; machine appliquéd; 42 x 45 inches (107 x 114 cm).

B. J. Adams
Washington, District of Columbia

Variations on "B"
Acrylic painted canvas embellished with actual items (bows and buttons) and heat-transferred images; machine embroidered; 42 x 42 inches (107 x 107 cm).

Variations on "B" is the second in a series using the alphabet as the theme and allowing one wall hanging for each letter. Butterflies, bananas, bows, brushes, buttons, and a baseball become the images for "B." The background was first painted and then pieced to receive the embroidered and heat-transferred subjects. A few bows and buttons were added for texture and depth, and the brushes have paint drifting from their bristles. Why not bones, buckles, or bread?

Connie Scheele
Houston, Texas

Early Autumn
Monoprinted and dye-painted cotton,
silk quilting threads; machine pieced
and hand quilted; 65 x 47 inches
(165 x 119 cm).

For many years my work has
been about things in nature:
river rocks, grasses, foliage, etc.
Instead of piecing the images
together, I have been exploring
monoprinting to create the
images in the fabric. This piece is
about walking through the
woods in the early autumn.

Moulting in itself is a fascinating process, but the fact that it allows us to get this close feel and touch of feathers makes it truly amazing. Finding the feathers in the birds' own environment adds a bit of reality for bird-watchers. We have tried to reflect this reality in our quilt.

Inge Mardal & Steen Hougs
Chantilly, France

Moulting
Hand-painted cotton; machine quilted;
75 x 56 inches (191 x 142 cm).

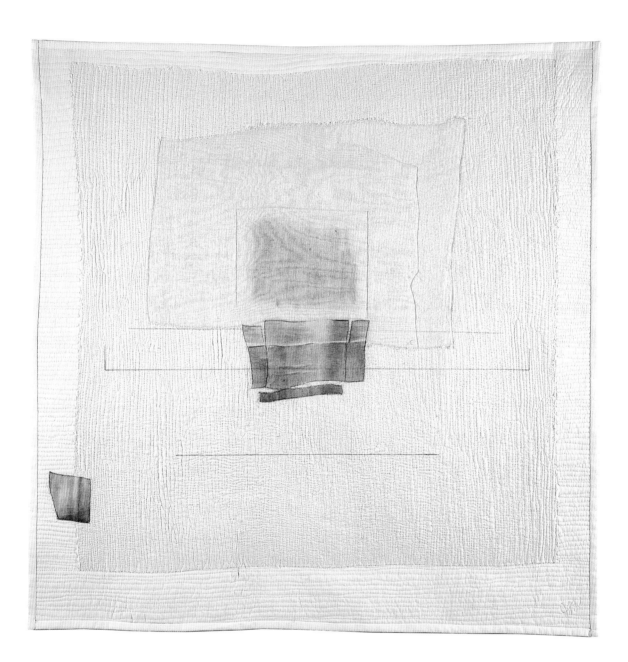

Jeanne Lyons Butler
Huntington, New York

White #2
Wool, silk, and cotton fabric; cotton
batting, rayon, cotton/polyester, nylon
threads; 42 x 42 inches (107 x 107 cm).

Stimulation comes from a desire for quiet and calm.
Looking for peace, blurring the high energy of daily
activity, allows me to take control.

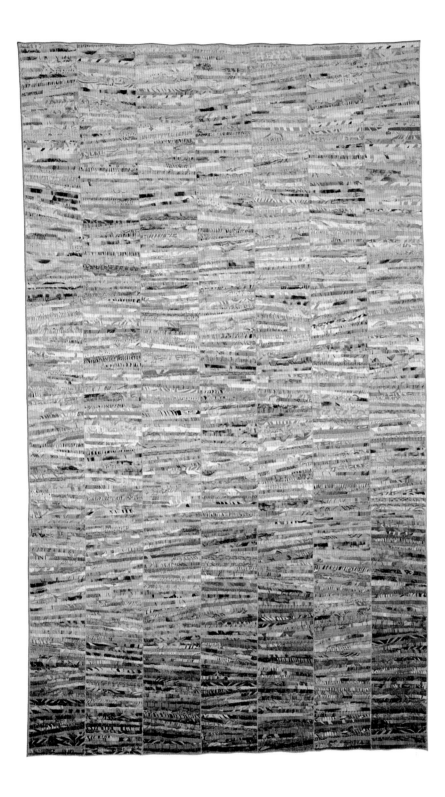

Judy Hooworth
Terrey Hills, New South Wales,
Australia

Road to Condo #2
Torn and layered cottons stitched
to cotton foundation; machine
stitched and quilted; 50 x 86
inches (127 x 218 cm).

Condobolin is a small town in the
center of New South Wales, and I
have travelled the beautiful country
road from Sydney on many occa-
sions over the years to visit my
favorite uncle and aunt. The last couple of trips were tinged with sadness
as my uncle was in ill health and
died before I could return. This quilt
is about my memories of the landscape's colors, and my emotional
response to the passing of an era.

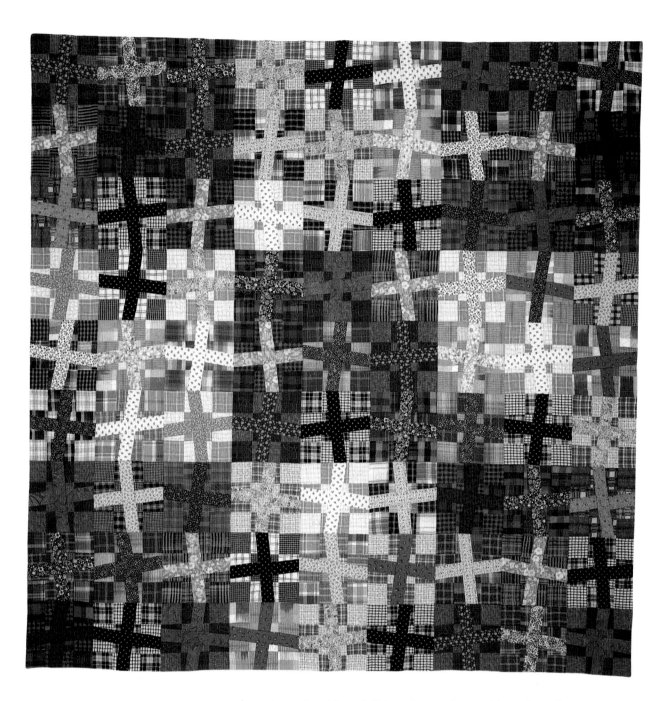

Ingrid Taylor
Fairbanks, Alaska

Dia de los Muertos
Cotton plaids and calicoes;
machine pieced and quilted;
60 x 60 inches (152 x 152 cm).

A long-time idea of slicing nine patches and inserting other fabrics finally came to fruition in this quilt. I was astounded that this simple approach to piecing could result in such complexity: all colors, old/new, small/large, traditional/innovative, simple/complex, static/dancing. The more I looked at the quilt, the more it suggested the joyful approach some cultures show towards death — the synthesis of life's experiences.

Ana Lisa Hedstrom
LaHonda, California

Riff II
Silk pique, shibori dyed
and discharged; pieced
and hand stitched; 47 x 69
inches (119 x 175 cm).

Indigenous American
music — blues, bluegrass,
folk, and especially jazz —
is often my working
companion in the studio.
There is a correlation
between the making of
music and the creation of
pieced quilts. My dyeing
and decision making are
improvisations of color,
form and line rhythm,
pauses, repeats, and variations. *Riff II* is part of a
series dedicated to our
inspiring legacy of jazz.

Lori Lupe Pelish
Niskayuna, New York

Injuries
Commercial cottons; machine
appliquéd, embroidered, and
quilted; 35 x 57 inches
(89 x 145 cm).

This quilt series revolves
around the family unit. The
structure of the family is
shaped and molded by life's
circumstances, alternately
strengthened or weakened
by these events.

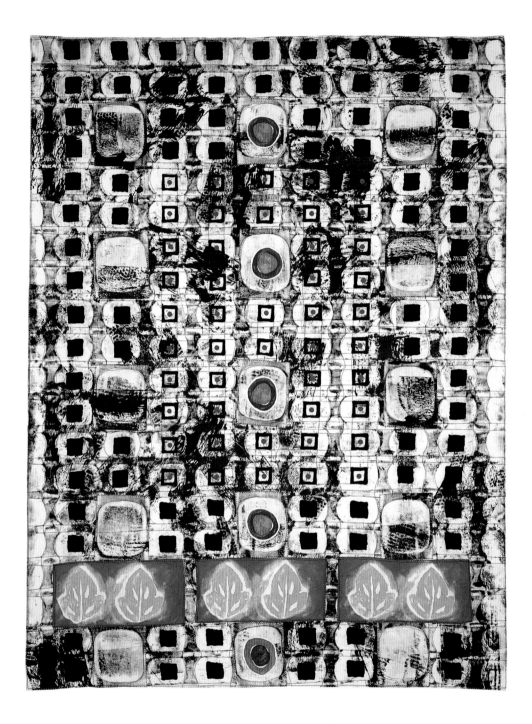

My work incorporates scrap fabric, hand-stamped shapes used to form collages, and the hand-printed textures of the orange construction fences that seem to surround construction sites these days. I am working to combine the grids of the construction fence with other building textures and repeats, or with nature that grows around the construction.

Jeanne Williamson
Natick, Massachusetts

Orange Construction Fence Series #6
100 percent cotton fabric, fabric paint, monoprinted textures of construction fences, hand stamped with rubber erasers; machine appliquéd and quilted; 31 x 40 inches (79 x 102 cm).

Domini McCarthy Memorial Award

Nelda Warkentin
Anchorage, Alaska

Tropical Dream
Multiple layers of painted silk organza on a
quilted cotton and linen base; machine
pieced and quilted; 48 x 60 (122 x 152 cm).

This quilt brings the viewer to the memory of a
favorite time and place, easily moving them into a
dream of visiting warm, carefree, tropical days that are
waiting just beyond the horizon. Letting your mind
bring you to a sense of serenity can feel so good.

I was a very young child, having my yearly school physical, and I saw the doctor write the initials F.L.K. in the margin of my medical chart. Many years later, I discovered that F.L.K. stood for Funny Looking Kid, a term given to perfectly healthy, normal children who look and act — well — funny. The image on the quilt is from a first-grade picture, taken right before it dawned on me just how funny looking I was.

Alison F. Whittemore
San Antonio, Texas

Funny Looking Kid (FLK)
100 percent cotton embellished with a gridded photograph drawn one square at a time; machine quilted; 37 x 52 inches (94 x 132 cm).

Camilla Brent Pearce
Pittsburgh, Pennsylvania

Lefferts Avenue Kuba I
Found fabrics; 9 x 12 inches
(23 x 30 cm).

In making *Lefferts Avenue Kuba I*, I was influenced by the African textiles that I saw frequently in my Brooklyn neighborhood. I wanted the formal challenge of juxtaposing the graphic quality of Kuba cloth with traditional American quilt patterns.

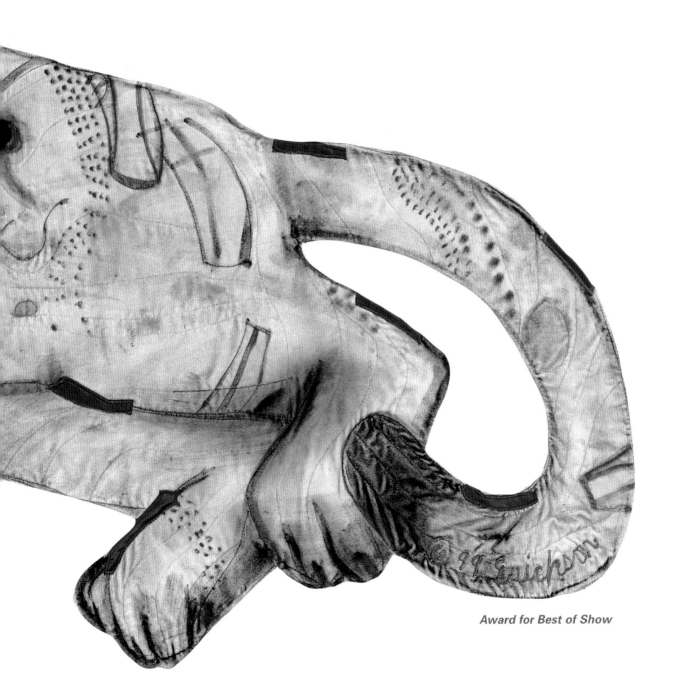

Award for Best of Show

Nancy N. Erickson
Missoula, Montana

Felis Forever (1)
Velvet, satin, cotton, felt (filler) fabric
paints, oil paintsticks; machine stitched and
appliquéd; 69 x 39 inches (175 x 99 cm).

In the mid 1990s I worked on quilted pieces that showed bears in caverns or in rooms formerly occupied by humans and covered with cave drawings of early animals. The bears wander through these environments, teaching their cubs about history. In this new series, *Felis...*, the ancient history is imprinted on the cougars; the cougars are freed of caves and rooms, and they move freely on the wall.

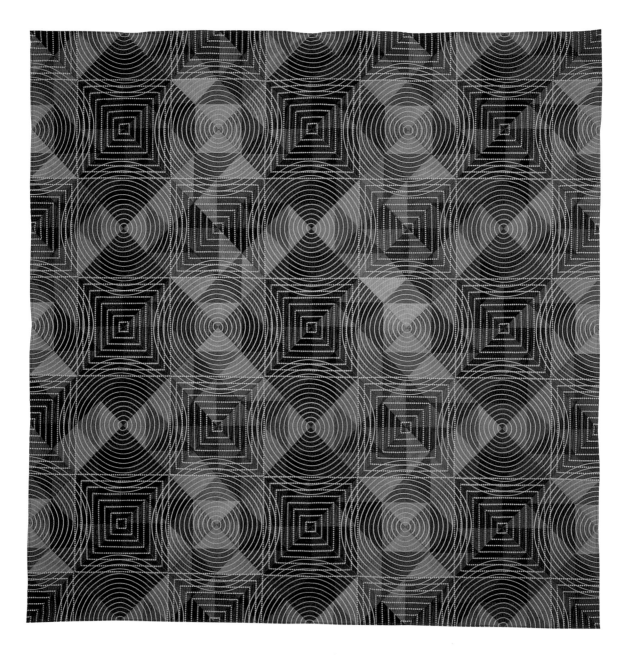

I have been working on this Block series for several years. They are composed of a series of 7 3/4-inch square blocks that are created by printing different patterns in both dyes and inks on fabric. I first draw the patterns on the computer, and then use the computer drawings to make photo emulsion silkscreens. There are many inconsistencies in the process and I am always surprised by the results.

Ellen Oppenheimer
Oakland, California

PW Block 4
Silk-screened dyes and inks on cotton; machine sewn, machine quilted; 66 x 66 inches (168 x 168 cm).

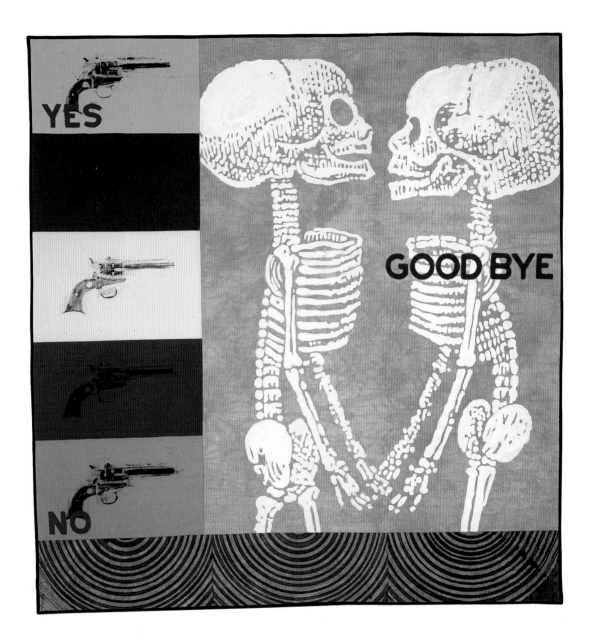

Bean Gilsdorf
Portland, Oregon

Ouija #1
CREAM (Cathy Rasmussen Emerging Artist Memorial) Award Sponsored by Studio Art Quilt Associates
Hand-dyed and commercial cotton fabrics, dyed, monoprinted, painted, and relief printed by the artist; machine pieced, appliquéd, quilted, and tied; 47 x 50 inches (119 x 127 cm).

Skeletons typically signify death, but for me they represent the essence of humanity. The visual elements in this quilt evolved from my fear and rage about violent events in my personal history and in American culture. While working on this quilt, I explored ideas about fate and precognition, using text from a Ouija board to evoke the indiscriminate nature of violence. This quilt is a warning, an amulet, and a private memorial.

About the Dairy Barn

The Dairy Barn Southeastern Ohio Cultural Arts Center is a unique arts facility in the Appalachian foothills. Its year-round calendar of events features both juried and curated exhibitions of work by regional, national, and international artists. In addition, the facility is the venue for festivals, performances, and a full range of classes for children and adults.

The history of the Dairy Barn is as colorful as its exhibits. Built in 1913, the structure housed an active dairy herd until the late 1960s. After sitting idle about 10 years, the building was scheduled for demolition. Fortunately, local artist Harriet Anderson and her husband, Ora, recognized the building's potential as a much needed regional arts center. They worked tirelessly to rally community support to save the dilapidated structure. With only nine days to spare, the demolition order was reversed, and the building was placed on the National Register of Historic Places. The Dairy Barn Southeastern Ohio Cultural Arts Center, a nonprofit organization, was born.

The architects retained the original character of the building through several renovation projects as it evolved from a seasonal, makeshift exhibit space into a first-class, fully accessible arts facility. Early 2001 saw the completion of a one million dollar renovation project. The ground level now houses a 6,600-square-foot exhibition space and a 400-square-foot retail gift shop that features work by regional and exhibiting artists. The formerly unused 7,000-square-foot upper level haymow now includes two large classroom spaces; three large multipurpose rooms suitable for classes, performances, and special events; offices for the staff; and storage space.

The Dairy Barn is supported by admissions, memberships, corporate sponsorships, grants, and donations. The staff is assisted by a large corps of volunteers who annually donate thousands of hours of time and talent. For a calendar of events and information about other Dairy Barn programs, contact the Dairy Barn Cultural Arts Center, P.O. Box 747, Athens, Ohio 45701, USA; phone, 740-592-4981; or visit the Internet site, www.dairybarn.org.

Show Itinerary

The complete Quilt National '03 collection will be on display from May 24 through September 1, 2003 at the Dairy Barn Southeastern Ohio Cultural Arts Center located at 8000 Dairy Lane in Athens, Ohio. Three separate groups of Quilt National '03 works (identified as Collections A, B, and C) will then begin a two-year tour to museums and galleries. Tentative dates and locations are listed below. It is recommended that you verify this information by contacting the specific host venue prior to visiting the site.

For an updated itinerary, or to receive information about hosting a Quilt National touring collection, contact the Dairy Barn Arts Center.

P.O. Box 747, Athens, Ohio, 45701
Phone: 740-592-4981
Email: artsinfo@dairybarn.org>artsinfo@dairybarn.org
Internet site: www.dairybarn.org>www.dairybarn.org

5/24 - 9/1/03	Athens, Ohio; Dairy Barn Cultural Arts Center [full collection]
10/22 - 11/30/03	St Louis, Missouri; The City Museum [A, B and C]
1/17 - 4/11/04	Asheville, North Carolina; Southern Highland Craft Guild [A]
4/1 - 4/4/04	Lancaster, Pennsylvania; Quilters' Heritage Celebration [C]
6/3 - 9/12/04	Delray Beach, Florida; Cornell Museum of Art and History [A]
9/4 - 10/16/04	Bloomingdale, Illinois; Bloomingdale Park District Museum [B]
3/31 - 4/3/05	Lancaster, Pennsylvania; Quilters' Heritage Celebration [A & B]
5/1 - 6/30/05	Fort Dodge, Iowa; Blanden Memorial Art Museum [C]

The Dairy Barn

Artists' Index